MICROCOSM PUBLISHING is Portland's most diversified publishing house and distributor, with a focus on the colorful, authentic, and empowering. Our books and zines have put your power in your hands since 1996, equipping readers to make positive changes in their lives and in the world around them. Microcosm emphasizes skill-building, showing hidden histories, and fostering creativity through challenging conventional publishing wisdom with books and bookettes about DIY skills, food, bicycling, gender, self-care, and social justice. What was once a distro and record label started by Joe Biel in a drafty bedroom was determined to be *Publishers Weekly*'s fastest-growing publisher of 2022 and #3 in 2023, and is now among the oldest independent publishing houses in Portland, OR, and Cleveland, OH. Biel is also the winner of PubWest's Innovator Award in 2024. We are a politically moderate, centrist publisher in a world that has inched to the right for the past 80 years.

CONTENTS

FRUGAL VEGAN'S HAPPY HOME

Crafts, Rituals & Recipes for Every Season

LISA VAN DEN BOOMEN

Microcosm Publishing
Portland, OR / Cleveland, OH

THE FRUGAL VEGAN'S HAPPY HOME

Crafts, Rituals, and Recipes for Every Season
Part of the DIY Series

First Edition, 3,000 copies
ISBN 9781648414534
This is Microcosm # 977
Designed by Sarah Koch and Joe Biel
Edited by Ivy Zeller

For a catalog, write or visit:
Microcosm Publishing
2752 N Williams Ave.
Portland, OR 97227

All the news from the misprints in print at www.Microcosm.Pub/Newsletter

Get more copies of this book at www.Microcosm.Pub/FrugalVegan

Did you know that you can buy our books directly from us at sliding scale rates? Support a small, independent publisher and pay less than Amazon's price at www.Microcosm.Pub.

To join the ranks of high-class stores that feature Microcosm titles, talk to your rep: In the U.S. **COMO** (Atlantic), **ABRAHAM** (Midwest), **BOB BARNETT** (Texas, Oklahoma, Arkansas, Louisiana), **IMPRINT** (Pacific), **TURNAROUND** (UK), **UTP/MANDA** (Canada), **NEWSOUTH** (Australia/New Zealand), **Observatoire** (Africa, Europe), **IPR** (Middle East), **Yvonne Chau** (Southeast Asia), **HarperCollins** (India), **Everest/B.K. Agency** (China), **Tim Burland** (Japan/Korea), and **FAIRE** in the gift trade.

Global labor conditions are bad, and our roots in industrial Cleveland in the 70s and 80s made us appreciate the need to treat workers right. Therefore, our books are MADE IN THE USA and printed on post-consumer paper.

Library of Congress Cataloging-in-Publication LCCN 2025041950

EU Safety Information: https://microcosmpublishing.com/gpsr

Medical Disclaimer: This book is not a substitute for medical advice. Please consult your health care professional(s) before trying remedies, dietary changes, etc. to discuss how they may interact with your body, any medications/supplements you may be on, and any other unique health needs you may have.

PUBLISHER'S NOTE

In 2004, we received a package from Canada. It contained a zine with lots of energy, festivities, and creativity. We let the author know that we were interested in republishing it in the U.S. and she sent a gleeful response. When we sent her a royalty check, she published a blog post about how awesome it was to get paid to make zines! She made more. We continued to work together. More mutual appreciation ensued.

This book started out as four zines in a classic nineties cut-and-paste style, with each page full of cheerful effusions in various fonts, pasted in at odd angles. When we decided to compile them into a book, the format posed a few challenges, primarily that the zine pages were different sizes. We realized we'd need to pull them apart and put them together again, while retaining the scrappy charm of the originals as best we could. You can judge the results for yourself.

We left the original contents as close as possible to the originals; we removed redundant instances of a few recipes and tips that appeared in multiple issues and cut some projects and recipes that were borrowed from early blogs where we couldn't verify the permissions. We removed URLs for expired websites but otherwise left the information as-is, even when it's patently out of date.

Those of you who were frugal vegans in Canada in the late nineties and early aughts may find the dollar amounts that appear in these pages comfortingly nostalgic; the rest of you may have your eyes pop out at just how frugal it seems, but we've preserved it as part of the lore. Things have changed in the economy more broadly! Eggs and avocados are no longer available at the bargain prices we once enjoyed. The restaurant The Spirite Lounge is no longer in business, but the review is so charming we didn't want to deprive you of it.

The world changes constantly, but the impulse to live lightly and joyfully upon it stays strong. Please take your inspiration from Lisa's exuberance and experience, even as you derive your own methods and wiles. We hope you'll keep a record of your own favorite methods to share with others.

FOREWORD

The book you are about to enjoy comprises a collection of zines created by Lisa Van Den Boomen, aka "The Frugal Vegan," my amazing late wife who left us far too soon.

Lisa was many things: a maple-syrup-loving Quebecer, a proud vegan, a free-spirited, witchy hippie, a polyglot, a humanitarian, an environmentalist, a soap maker, a foodie, a coffee nerd, and an animal lover with a relentless drive and passion for making this world just a little bit of a better place to live in for all creatures, big and small.

The zines initially served as a creative outlet and a way to promote veganism at a time when vegan alternatives were not as readily available as they are today. The frugal part was out of necessity at some points, but also to let people know that not everything in life has to be expensive or cost money at all. "I can make that myself" was always one of her favorite things to say in my native Dutch (*kan ik zelf maken*), and she sought to empower her readers to do the same.

I am so proud that her message continues to live on and resonate with people all over the world and is now available in book form. Flip through the pages, browse a specific section, read it cover to cover, but most of all, enjoy the many recipes, frugal tips, projects, crafts, and gift ideas, which are still as relevant and useful as ever.

A big thank-you to Microcosm and to you, dear reader. Any author royalties for this book will be donated to Microcosm's worker snack fund, as well as an animal shelter in Portland.

I hope you will love this collection as much as Lisa loved creating it.

—Walter Van Den Boomen (aka Dutchie)

Spring and Summer

INTRODUCTION

Spring and summer are times of rest, rejuvenation, and rebirth. To celebrate that energy, in the pages ahead you'll find frugal and vegan tips and recipes to brighten the warmer seasons.

FRUGAL ACTIVITIES AND TIPS

Spring Cleaning

Cleaning 101

It all starts here. What better way to start this book than with some good cleaning advice?

Okay, I'll admit it, I'm not the best housekeeper and my cleaning skills are mediocre but I do know how to do it, how to make great cleansers, and how things should be done! I'm just not good at carrying these tasks out myself.

If you really don't like cleaning and throwing crap out, invite a friend over to help motivate you. Barter with them, feed them food and liquor so they will want to help.

The best thing to do is concentrate on one room at a time. Start with small rooms like your bathroom. It might be gross and grimy but cleanup will be relatively quick, assuming you cleaned it a few times in the past few months!

I find when my house gets messy everywhere I get overwhelmed and don't want to clean anything at all. *Where to start??*

Even if you do one room one day, and another the next, it makes things less scary.

Throw Stuff Out, Darn-It!

Okay people (yes, I'm talking to you packrats), remember that part of cleaning is throwing shit out. If you haven't used something in over a year, or there's shampoo sitting there in tiny bottles you stole from the hotel that no one is using . . . THROW IT OUT! If the items are still good, keep 'em . . . but for someone else.

What I do is keep a box in one room and when I clean a room and find stuff I don't want anymore, I just put it in that box. Once the box looks full, I decide whether I want to have a yard sale, donate to friends or organizations, or post it on Freecycle.org (YOU MUST go there).

Don't keep clothes either. I am really bad at this but getting better. I buy used clothes a few times a month. There's stuff I love but don't wear. (I'm planning a big cleanout soon, I swear!)

A good way to get rid of clothes is to have a clothes swap: invite everyone over who also has used clothes to toss and just dump all the clothes in a pile—go nutty. Remember, no fighting or pulling your friends' hair. If you and your friend like the same item, share it!

Just don't be afraid to throw stuff out. They are only THINGS, things are not important are they? (Okay, but keep your zines!)

How to Make Spring Cleaning Fun and Not Suck

I don't know about you, but any sentence which includes the word *cleaning* in it just makes me wanna cry and cringe at the same time. I am not good at all at mundane tasks. I fail at them!

But why are you going to listen to my advice? Because I am one of you. You're not going to get a Martha Stewart advice book nor will I tell you how to perfectly organize and label everything in your house.

So if you're thinking that you might want to start cleaning and decluttering soon, here are a few tips on how to make it fun and not suck too bad:

1. **Set the mood.** Cleaning is like work to me. We all go to work and have some kind of routine. For example, before you tackle your daily tasks, you might read the paper, drink your coffee, and perhaps chat to a colleague. Or you might listen to your favorite music, maybe check your email—I kind of call it "Setting the Mood." In a sense, we need to do a few enjoyable activities before tackling less enjoyable ones, making things easier on a balance.

   Same goes for cleaning. Set the mood! My partner put on Michael Jack's Greatest Hits and was blasting it right before I started! At first, I laughed and questioned his odd choice, but after a couple of songs, I found myself laughing at the cheesy songs and remembering those from when I was a kid. Soon enough, I was in a fun mood and somewhat in the mood to scrub

faster. Music is always a good motivator . . . just pick something good . . . or even bad.

2. **Pick one space to clean.** The last thing you want to do is start cleaning one room, then jump to the next because you're getting bored or frustrated with the first one. Trust me, I've done it. Not only will you feel like nothing is getting done, but you likely won't accomplish a whole lot.

   Don't overwhelm yourself, this stuff doesn't get accomplished in an hour. Pick one room to focus on cleaning . . . even if it's the smallest room. Then pick a corner where you'll start. If you set aside ten to thirty minutes, you will feel better already. Baby steps people, seriously it works! Just don't go in all gung-ho or you'll have that problem with being overwhelmed.

3. **Clean or organize?** I often fail to organize or clean my organization at the same time. Can you tell I'm not blessed with being able to multitask that great? (If you can, that's awesome.)

   I prefer to sort my items that I don't need at all and clean my place once everything is organized. However, not everyone is like me.

   If you want to get rid of clutter first, sort out your items beforehand and organize.

   If you're good at organizing items together while cleaning at the same time, then that's great! Sometimes it's difficult if you haven't done these things in years or forever though, to achieve organization through cleaning.

   What helps me is that I make piles of my items and put them in boxes where they need to go —have a donation pile, keep pile, and sell pile.

   You might find it's also best to keep a decluttering goal in mind. For instance, maybe you only want to donate

two garbage bags this week for a charity, for example. Or maybe you sort your items, but not do anything else.

Earth Day Ideas

I won't spend too much time talking about Earth Day. I am sure everyone is already being bombarded with articles, events, and rants related to this topic. There shouldn't have to be an Earth Day: we should all be contributing daily. Here are a few easy things you can do today (and preferably every day)!

1. **Eat a vegetarian/vegan meal. I know there are meat** eaters amongst my readers so I wanted to mention it). If meat eaters made a commitment to eat vegetarian meals two to three times a week, they'd be making a BIG difference.
2. **Leave your car at home.** Walk, rollerblade, skateboard, take public transit, or cycle to work as much as you can. If you must take your car, try to get at least four to five people to drive with you.
3. **Bring your own containers and mug.** If you like to drink takeout coffee and food, bring your own containers and mug. I recently discovered that the Starbucks tumblers never leak. I haven't found another one quite so amazing. I got it for free after telling them I forgot my own mug and couldn't find one at the dollar store; therefore they decided to give me a large soy latte and the mug, free of charge. Not sure how I scored that.
4. **Host a craft party.** Make cool stuff using recyclable items or make your own green homemade cleaners to share.
5. **Donate money.** Find a non-profit organization such as WWF, Greenpeace, or a local organization which helps protect the environment.

6. **Pick up trash.** Walk around your local park or neighborhood and pick up trash! Clean up our nasty streets.
7. **Unplug everything in your house.** Disconnect anything that you don't use on a daily basis. You wouldn't believe the money and energy saved.
8. **Eat dinner by candlelight.** Extra points: do this while listening to the radio! I use my Eton crank radio, but you can use any radio with rechargeables! Make sure to turn off all the lights and electronics in your house too.

HAPPY EARTH DAY EVERYONE!!

Ways to Save Money

Not Buying New

A group in San Francisco started this a couple of years ago: a commitment not to purchase anything new (besides toiletries, food, and any consumable items) for one year. When I first read the article, I was very interested in doing this but didn't make the commitment until now. Apparently, many of the people in the group were able to pay off loans because of this!

I started the venture a few weeks ago, mainly because I am unemployed and between contracts. Sometimes I find it difficult to walk in stores and find things I need but can't buy because they are new. I needed a pressure cooker to preserve some of my garden veggies. New ones were anywhere from $40+, and I found a really good old used one for $15—very solid and also came with the manual! My food processor cracked and I wanted another one. Took me three weeks to find an affordable one online for $10. Works great.

It has now become a challenge to find things that I am looking for, yet once I find them, I am more than pleased with my efforts, and my wallet is happy too! I had my ex-partner doing the same thing; his brother was coming for a visit and he didn't have any sheets or comforter for the futon in his living room. We went to the thrift store, and he purchased a heavy good quality comforter, flat sheet, and fitted sheet for about $10! Had he bought this all new, he would have spent well over $100 based on the quality of the stuff he bought. I also told my partner to come to me if he needed anything specific, and before he would run out and buy it, I would try and find it used.

Mind you, I had a slip up . . . kind of. I wanted three specific books and made a very serious attempt at purchasing them all used online, yet I didn't find any of them! I had received a gift card for a bookstore and got them this way . . . technically, it wasn't my money spent on the books since I got the card as a gift. At least that's how I convinced myself to do it! These were also books that were not available at the library so I was out of luck.

If you think you'd have a tough time with this, start by purchasing some used items, mainly larger purchases such as bicycles, furniture, appliances . . . feel less guilty and look for deals. You can even find stuff like used paint. A lot of people paint in their homes and have leftovers they don't need. This might be a good way to get free/cheap paint for a small room!

When buying larger appliances, make sure they are not too old as these would take up a lot of electricity, which would make your electric bill go up! You can probably purchase as old as ten to fifteen years as most of these are energy efficient.

When to make exceptions: Some things are not meant to be purchased used, or at least be careful if you do. I practice yoga often and needed a mat. I considered purchasing someone's old one and cleaning it, but clearly, there can be an issue with this as people can sweat A LOT during yoga depending on what type they practice, of course. In this case, I did buy a new one that came with a DVD and case so I could also practice at home, therefore saving me money on studio classes.

As a vegan, I prefer not to purchase used kitchen items that have had meat on/in them. If you do end up purchasing used pans, make sure to thoroughly clean or even bleach some of the parts so that no bacteria is left behind!

Ways to Save on Groceries

Buy stuff from discounted racks. If you don't see anything, ask the produce or bakery manager for old stuff. I've gone into bakeries and received free day-old bread and pita before, just ask!!

Check flyers from two to three supermarkets. Write down what you need and where it's cheaper or on sale.

Get no-name/generic brands. There is rarely a big difference in taste on most things.

Buy dried beans instead of canned. This will save you tons. Also get soymilk powder, especially if it goes quickly in your house. Use a blender to mix it.

Buy in bulk when possible. If you don't have the cash up front, have a few friends go in on larger boxes/bags of staple foods (rice, pasta, beans, flour, etc.). For example, I buy ten pounds of basmati for $9 as opposed to one pound for $3! Rice goes quickly in my house so this is worth the investment!

Getting Fit on a Budget

It's that time of year when everyone is running around panicking because soon they'll have to wear shorts or a bathing suit. Exercise is also great for the mind. I started because I was dealing with the stress of the loss of my father and it helped me tremendously. Here are some tips to get yourself in shape without costing a fortune.

Gyms

Gyms are horribly expensive but usually have summer deals. If you are determined to join a gym, go in several of them and see if they will give you a week's pass for free (most places will do this). You can accumulate free weeks of free gym time if you visit three to four gyms in your area. Afterwards, let the gym know you're low on funds and that you want the best deal. Compare. Sometimes if you tell one gym the other gym is going to give you a better deal, they'll make their price better. It can happen! So wheel and deal with gyms otherwise you'll end up spending a small fortune. Also check out the Y and university gyms. Those usually have decent summer rates.

Frugal Exercise

If you decide not to join a gym but still want to get fit:

Buy or acquire a decent bike. (Try Freecycle.org.) Bike to work, bike to school. Bike to the store and carry your groceries. It's a simple workout.

Walk everywhere. Walk as many places as you can. Climb stairs instead of taking the elevator.

Do more chores around the house that require lots of physical work (such as vacuuming or scrubbing).

Garden! Take an hour after work to pull weeds, shovel some dirt, and perhaps mow the lawn.

Recycle old bottles with good handles and fill them with water to use as weights.

Buy a used or free treadmill, stationary bike, or elliptical. Set it up at home and do thirty minutes three times a week. Definitely cheaper than going to a gym!

Frugal Yoga

Most **yoga** studios will either give you a free intro class or offer a "first-time" fee for about $10. This is a good way to try out different yoga places in your area. Most communities also have classes set up for about $50 for once a week for about eight weeks. These programs are usually sponsored by the local government, so look in your community guides.

Many studios offer what is called a "Community" Class. I've noticed this is offered in several cities I have been to and usually run about $5 a class for ninety minutes. I've even found FREE yoga in one city followed by a meditation and free veggie meal. These are usually offered by either religious organizations or community spiritual groups.

If you are on a limited budget, inquire about your options and let them know. You'd be surprised, some places might give you a few extra classes if you purchase a punch card or sign up for a class.

Buying a Yoga Mat

At first I looked for a free mat on Freecycle but had no luck there. In the end, I decided to purchase a mat/carrying case and DVD for $30. Seems a bit pricey at first, but since I can not afford to attend yoga classes more than once a week, I use the DVD for other days, which has wonderful 20 minute workouts.

Yoga Tip

Make sure that you don't eat 2 hours before going to a yoga class. Don't go to class hungry though, so if you must eat something, try a banana!

Quick and Cheap Decorating Ideas

1. **Paint.** Painting a room is the least expensive way to decorate a room if you want to make a drastic change. Get discounted paints that have been mistinted; they are always available. Also, paint old furniture that needs a fresh look. Paint is your friend . . . remember that.
2. **Plants.** I bought a couple of plants, then put clippings in water for a few weeks and planted them. A $5 investment has now produced over 10 plants for me. Also ask friends/family for clippings. My house is full of plants now and it looks so much cozier!
3. **Candles.** Get dollar store ones. Get holders at the thrift store. I have candles everywhere. It's an inexpensive way to bring ambience to a room. You can also melt leftover wax and pour it in a glass jar with a wick!
4. **Reupholster.** Make old grungy furniture new again with unused quilt covers using a staple gun and dye cushions. I revamped an old couch for $3 doing this. Wicked.
5. **De-Clutter/Clean.** Use baskets to store loose things. Then, clean and make the room smell good. Make a spritzer using a bit of vodka, water, and some essential oils as a freshener. Tidying a room can change a room's look, trust me on that one!

6. **Dress windows.** If you have bare windows, get some curtain clips (less than $5) and some fabric (sheets, tea towels, thrift store finds . . .). Clip the fabric on, then hang on a rod.

   I have bought smaller curtain rods at dollar stores before. You can also make your own curtain clips by either painting wooden laundry clips, using metal ones, or using plastic ones in the color you need.

   Attach a wire line in front of your window and clip on fabric.

Saving a Few Bucks a Day

There are tons of ways to save a few bucks a day. Some of you who have been broke for a long time probably know these tips, and some are really obvious, but for those who want them anyway, here they are:

1. **Take the bus/walk/ride your bike.** I live in town. Winters I have to take the bus, but when it warms up, I can walk downtown. It takes me a little longer, but it saves me a few bucks! Also keeps me in decent shape too.
2. **Carpool.** I used to work in the middle of nowhere and didn't have the option to carpool because I worked different hours than most people in the office. However, carpooling rocks if you can swing it. Post ads at your workplace! This saves people gas money, and it's also better for the environment. Lots of people at my work did it.
3. **Bring food with you.** Being vegan is tough sometimes. We can't really buy a lot of baked goods that are out there. If you're planning on meeting a friend for coffee, bring your own snack! Even if there are things I can eat, I try to avoid it if possible. Baked goods at coffee places are not cheap. I also carry food in case I can't go

home for whatever reason. I carry fruit leather on me, as well as goods that won't go bad. If you get snack-y, just reach into your bag instead of walking in a grocery store or corner store for a last-minute snack.

4. **Find cheap entertainment.** The library is the coolest place to get free entertainment; you can rent videos, CDs, tapes, and of course books! Don't spend your hard-earned cash on rented videos and movie theaters (unless it's a film festival).

   Or throw a potluck! This is one of my favorite activities. There is always an abundance of yummy creations at your disposal. Most people leave their leftovers behind, so you'll most likely end up with free food for a week.

   Most cities and even towns have festivals. Lots of free stuff to do! Check your listings. Summer is the time for cities to have all kinds of festivals and free live music outdoors!

   Host a craft party. Ask everyone to bring a craft they can teach, and everyone gets to make stuff! I used to go to a lot of these! They are sometimes called: Stitch and Bitch parties!

   Or take up knitting. I know, knitting isn't one of those summer crafts, but at the rate I knit it takes me a while to finish anything. If you're like me and are not a pro at it, make scarves because they are super easy. Make sure to use cotton or acrylic wool. You can knit through the summer and once fall/winter comes, you have a stash of scarves you can give as gifts to friends and family.

Cool Ass Frugal Gifts

Awesome Magnets

This is the neatest and easiest craft and SO cheap! I've given the gifts to people who were super impressed, and it looks so fancy! Here's what you'll need:

- A bag of clear bubbled-looking glass pieces
- Cutouts of pictures
- Scissors or craft punch
- Gel super glue
- Magnet pieces

Instructions:

First, find a nice picture you want to make into a magnet. Make sure it's small/big enough for your magnet.

Trace around the picture using your glass piece. Cut around a little smaller than your tracing. Make sure it fits behind the glass piece! Place the picture face side up against the flat side of the glass piece to make sure it fits. Look through the bubbled side to see how it's going to look when it's glued into place.

Put a tiny amount of super glue on the flat side of the glass bead. Spread out with a piece of cardboard so you don't get big chunks of glue showing through! Carefully place the picture against the glue and hold for a second.

Glue on a piece of magnet, and voilà! These look SO cool! You can design your own graphics and even make vegan magnets for friends. I made some nice 1" cat magnets for my mom and my friend's mom for Mother's Day, which cost me about 50¢ each! They loved them because they are unique!

Other magnets: You can also make other magnets out of recycled items such as beer or pop bottle caps, buttons, or any other small item. Scope out the thrift store for neat stuff!

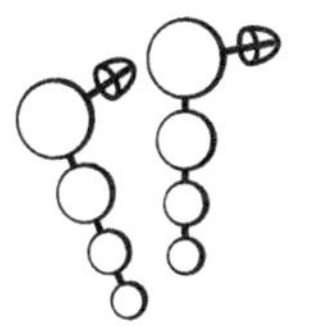

Earrings

You can make funky earrings out of buttons and other small items. Go to your local bead store and buy those pierced earring metal things you can glue on the back! Use metal wire to make hoops with beads!

Gummi Kebabs

These are SO cool. All you have to do is take some bamboo skewers and put some vegan gummi-type candies on them (different shapes and sizes). I usually wrap each kebab with a sandwich bag and decorate with stickers and ribbon.

You can also use some of that styrofoam stuff they use for flower arrangements, put it in a long mug, and stick the kebabs in there, then wrap with cello. Makes a cool bouquet!

I once made a cone for a friend of mine filled with these kebabs. He loved it! I paid $5 for candies and made about twenty kebabs! This can make two large candy bouquets or four small ones. Coolest gift ever for the candy lover or kids.

Candy Bouquets

I have seen these everywhere. People send them for gifts instead of flowers. They are really cool but A LOT of work. I've done one before and it took so long that I never made another one. After my easy gummi bouquet project, I decided to give another crack at the candy bouquet but make it EASY and fast. Perhaps it's just that I am not a perfectionist. I want things done fast, and I want everything to look cool. So here is MY version of a fast candy bouquet. Here's what you'll need:

- Pipe cleaners (various colours)
- Wrapped candies or lollipops (various colours, shapes, and types)

- Bamboo skewers
- Flower arranging foam
- A mug, jar, or painted recycled tin can

Instructions:
Okay, if you wanna save money, split the bamboo skewers in half if they are really long. Take half of the skewer and a candy. Take the loose wrapper part and pinch it with the skewer. Take a pipe cleaner and wrap around the candy/skewer a few times and a bit down the skewer. I use an entire pipe cleaner per stick but I suppose you could cut them in half. I just like it to go a bit further down the skewer. So there is your first "candy flower." Keep going until you have as many as you need.

Take your mug/tin, then cut a chunk of flower arranging foam so that it's a bit bigger than inside the mug. Squish it inside! Don't worry—this stuff will fit in! Stick all your prepared candy flowers inside. If you want, you could probably stuff in some fake grass to fill the gaps in the mug. I just left it the way it is, but you can use your imagination to pretty it up! I would say a twenty-four candy bouquet would cost about $2 maximum depending on where you get your supplies. Most people have leftover candy or mugs kicking around the house. (Or ask grandma!)

Saving On Back-to-School Stuff

Whether you are a parent or going back to school yourself, there are numerous ways you can save money on school items:

Buy paper, pens, and other usable goods cheaply at dollar stores—or in bulk, splitting the cost with friends/family.

Reuse existing binders you have or go to thrift stores; they usually have some. Or post an ad on Freecycle.org (your local chapter) to request some.

Find out if any textbooks you need are available used. Place ads in school, look online as well!

Get fall clothes at thrift stores or yard sales. There are usually a lot of yard sales at the end of the summer.

Buy used thermoses to store coffee, tea, or soup. I know when I was in school, I spent too much on "to go" coffee; this is a great way to save! Soup also keeps warm a long time—great for lunches.

Reuse existing backpacks (book bags) or find others at thrift stores.

If you need a computer, there are many used ones for sale that work great. My sweetie sold his laptop for $250, and it was a pretty good one! Also, look for sales with major computer companies as they often offer back-to-school specials for students. If you purchase online with major companies, they usually offer discounts if you have a student card. Don't put yourself in debt to buy a computer; there are many fantastic ones out there as so many people replace their computers on a regular basis.

Make a list of necessities and stick to it. We often like to reward ourselves and kids with things when it's time to go back to school—funky pens, trendy accessories—just buy what's on the list of what you need, and you'll save money.

Wait to buy. Right before school, everything is expensive because retailers know you need it. If you have to purchase anything new/retail, wait till school has started, then buy. After the first few weeks, retailers put all their school supplies on sale.

HAPPY STUDIES!

Thrift Store Tips

Check if what you want to buy needs to be dry cleaned or has extra maintenance involved. Sometimes you can hand wash dry clean items, but sometimes you can't. The price might be right, but if you have to get it dry cleaned often, it can be a costly purchase.

Check for possible holes or rips in clothes. I know it's a thrift store, but sometimes you can get discounts at the cash register if you point them out. You might not get a discount for a missing button, but try anyway. Usually, cashiers are fairly laidback, and going to smaller thrift stores (as opposed to chain ones) is better as they have more flexibility to change prices.

Try not to set out to find something specific. Having this mindset, you might miss out on other things that would look great. Every time I have tried consciously looking for something, I never found it. I've always had the best finds when I've gone in there not really searching for anything. Keep an open mind!

Check for stains. Some stains can be removed, but some can't. I've gotten almost free clothes at the store because they weren't sure if the stains would come out. The cashiers where I go seem pretty knowledgeable. If the stain can come out, you probably won't get a discount, but if they are unsure, you'll get the item for free or almost nothing.

Don't buy something if you are not 100% sure. I've bought things because it was cheap: "Oooooooooh, $2 for this top!!" It would fit okay but not great, and because I may have liked the pattern, I would buy it. I might wear something like that once, then toss it.

Only buy something if you look in the mirror and go, "WOW." You'll save yourself a lot of money. We tend to be more cautious with a more expensive purchase, but when something is cheap, we lower our standards. You deserve the best, so just get things you simply adore.

Frugal Polyamorous Dating  

When we have more than one partner and have to go on more than a few dates, things can get pricey if you're going out to dinner, movies, or any type of outings on a regular basis. It's possible to do romantic things and have special dates with everyone without spending much money. Here are some ideas, which can also be good for monogamous people too of course!

Cook dinner for your special sweetie.

Take a walk in a park or in the city, bring a thermos of coffee and freshly baked goods, and sit on a nice bench, talk, and enjoy the scenery. If you live close to a beach, this would be nice on a blanket too, right on the sand near the water.

In the summer, most places have lots of festivals going on. Check out what is happening in your town. We have a free buskers festival, a fringe festival which has plays for as low as $3, and a jazz festival which has free lunchtime concerts.

Rent a movie (or download one!) and make some popcorn and herbal tea.

Go to the library, take out a book of poetry or foreign literature, sit outside, and read to each other.

Lots of farms let you "Pick Your Own" fruits/veggies. This can be a nice date for people to share. Pick your own berries or fruits together, take them home, and make something with them.

Rent bikes (or use your own) and find bike trails in your area. Bring a picnic so you can stop along the way and rest to eat together; don't forget a blanket!

Ways to Make Money

How to Earn a Few Bucks

Okay, you're broke and need ways to make a few dollars to survive. Here are some great ideas:

Go dumpster diving or walk around on trash day and pick things up you can sell. Have a yard sale with all things you've found, plus some crap you want to get rid of! There are some great websites on dumpster diving, so if you wanna know more, do some research on the net.

Sell your skills! Have a talent? Can you clean? Decorate? Paint? Mow lawns? Garden? Are you handy around the house? Your talents can earn you a few bucks. Place signs around town with services you can offer! I once had a friend who could decorate people's homes with things they had lying around the house and just a few cans of paint. She was very popular because she recycled their unused items and people ended up with a completely designed house, and it didn't cost them a fortune! If you're artistic, this would be fantastic! I wish I still knew her because my place needs a little decorating.

Try button making. I invested in a button machine a few months ago and started selling buttons online with my own messages and designs. The key is to have UNIQUE buttons. Make sure others are not selling the same stuff as you. I haven't made a fortune, but it has earned me a few bucks that I needed. Check online for inexpensive button-making machines. The handheld ones are the cheapest but not good for volume. (If you're not planning to make hundreds, this option might be a good one to get though, as it's cheap.) I have the 1 ½–inch one, but I think people prefer the 1-inch one. It's just harder to get cheap parts for that (in my experience).

Do some spring cleaning and sell your junk on craigslist.com. You might even find some loose change while you're at it!

Have a yard sale but get your friends to participate too. The more stuff you have, the more people you will attract. Make cool flyers.

Go garbage picking in cities in the spring. Students are moving out and throw out tons of good stuff (trust me, I know). Keep what you need, sell what you don't. Repaint, wash, or restore sketchy things to earn a few more bucks on it.

Bake stuff. Can you bake? Sell vegan baked goods at your local flea market! Here we have a farmer's market with expensive tables to rent, so selling at the flea market is cheaper and there are less people with food there. People are always hungry at 8:00 AM and are in dire need of a coffee! Where I live, you don't need to have a food permit to sell baked goods at a market. My friend and I are currently revamping some recipes so we can start selling! Serve organic coffee with your goods! Place soy milk in an insulated lunch bag filled with ice packs to keep it cold. Offer a discount to those who bring their own coffee mug too! Use some of the baked goods recipes in this book. The great thing about selling food at flea markets is that not many people do. Most people sell tables of old stuff so your table will stand out and people will follow the coffee smell!

Walk the streets for cans/bottles. A lot of people in my neighborhood do this, so I know I wouldn't find much myself. However, if you live in a place where you can get cash back for empty bottles and cans, you can find these in LOTS of places. Scout busy streets after restaurants/stores have closed. Scan the garbage cans for empties. This won't make you rich but you might be able to buy yourself some food with your earnings.

Bring clothing to consignment shops. You'll get more from this than selling clothes at your yard sale. (I cover more about how to do this in a later section in this book.)

Sell books/DVDs/CDs. Lots of used stores accept books, DVDs, and CDs. You might not get a whole lot of money for them, but it's an easy way to get money on the spot.

Post items to sell on websites or newspapers. Most towns have a bargain hunter newspapers where you can list for free, and you can also sell online.

Sell things you make that you never thought you could sell. Do you have a big garden full of veggies and fruits? Sell some of your produce, jams, or if you have lots of plants, sell those too. You can also sell house plants using clippings. Spider plants are easy to grow! You can also sell the seeds you collect from your garden flowers. I usually collect my Lupin seeds and make packets from them.

Rent out your room/floor space. If you have a little extra room in your house/apartment, consider renting out the space to backpackers for a few bucks a night. If there are very strict laws about this where you live, you might want to be careful where you post ads. You can approach backpacker places in your area and give them your number if their hostel is full, which can happen during the summer months. If you have space, consider renting out your shed, attic, or garage for temporary storage space (say students are leaving town for the summer and need to store some boxes). Make sure your charges are less than the storage lockers in your town and trust your gut on the person you rent to. It'd be preferable just to rent it out for a few months/weeks so you don't have to deal with a long-term commitment.

How to Hold a Successful Yard Sale

Spring and summer are the best times to hold yard sales. You can get rid of all the crap you don't need (trust me, there's A LOT one doesn't need!) and make a few extra bucks. Here are a few tips:

Don't hold a yard sale to make money: have the mindset that someone is paying you to get rid of your junk. If you're selling something valuable or personal because you're broke, you won't succeed. Price stuff really low!

Don't bargain with people until the end of the day. If someone is persistent, tell them to come back later and if the item is still around they can have it for a better price.

Make colourful signs on main streets near where you live. Make it easy for people to find you!

Print out small flyers and place them in businesses around town. It's cheaper than placing an ad in the paper. It really works! Tell everyone you

know you're having a yard sale, including coworkers. Word gets around fast!

Also, try listing it on an e-group. My fave e-group is Freecycle. Check out freecycle.org and sign up for the Freecycle list in your city.

Clean all clothes and separate them by type (i.e., shirts, skirts, pants,etc.). A lot of people don't like ruffling through tons of clothes when it's not organized. They won't bother. You'll lose sales if you have a hundred pieces of clothes in one place.

Clean all appliances REALLY well. I once sold an old toaster oven for $10 because it was cleaned so it looked new. The people didn't hesitate to pay the asking price because it looked as if I really took care of it. (Yeah right, there was so much crap on there it took me an hour to clean it! Haha.) It's amazing how much better a super clean item will sell, and how much more it'll sell for. Again, this isn't about making tons of cash, but making the most with what you have.

If you have tons of mugs (like I do) price them individually but give people a discount if they buy more. I priced mine at 25¢ each but if they bought five, it was only $1. The key is to get rid of all your junk. This is a good way to do that.

Don't leave small items and knickknacks just lying around on a table. It looks like you're selling junk. Group some similar items in bags and price them. For example, I had tons of those Mardi Gras bead necklaces. I put them all in a bag and sold them for a buck. I also had tons of magnets which I put in a bag and priced for $4 (there were forty-three of them!) and wrote "good for collectors" on it because there were tons of weird magnets and some from businesses that don't exist anymore. Other small junk that can't be grouped can be placed in a small box, then sell every item in there for the same price.

Try to invite your friends to sell their stuff too. The more stuff you have, the more people will stop while driving by.

Place big stuff like furniture and vacuums near the front—to catch people's eye.

Timing is everything. I find the best time for me to hold a yard sale is late August. I live in a university town and lots of students are moving back to the city. Lots of students need stuff to furnish their apartment. Lots of people hold sales at this time as well, which means more people are driving/walking around looking for yard sales.

Last but not least: Make sure you have lots of change on hand!

How to Make Money from Consignment Shops

You can usually get more money for your used clothing from consignment shops. I took all the "designer" clothing I had bought (usually from thrift stores) and took them to the local consignment shops. I had bought a vintage seventies Geoffrey Bean Dress for $1 in Prince Edward Island in a thrift store which I kept for a few years. I never wore it because it didn't fit me quite right but I did love it. Took it to the consignment shop, it sold within an hour of me bringing it in and I got $20! Not bad for a $1 investment. I thought about posting it online but knew I was going to get more for it this way.

The key to consignment shops is that your clothes have to be very clean and mended; make sure they look the best they can

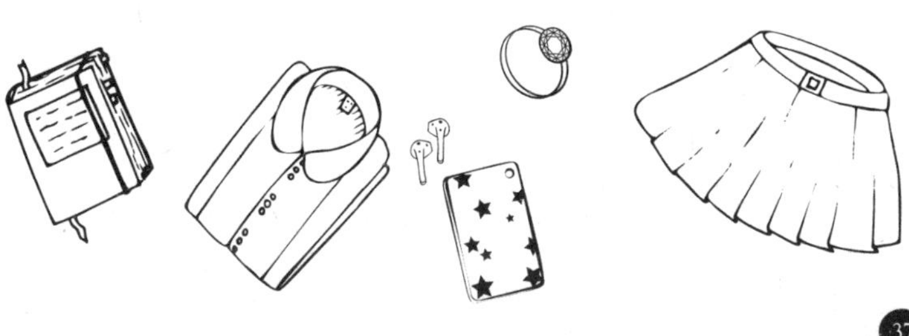

be before bringing them in. Most consignment shops where I live only take either very groovy vintage clothing or designer stuff.

Another thing you can do is go to the thrift store and if you find something from a very expensive designer, buy it and then go to a consignment shop to resell. Make sure the piece is also unique. Also, find out what the stores around you are looking for. The owners of the stores where I am are quite picky when it comes to taking anything. Ask first before you bring your clothes. Seems to be if the item is normally extremely pricey in the store (i.e. stuff like Marc Jacobs, Prada, etc.), then they usually take it. Or if it has a very unique style.

If you bring in clothes once a month, you could make a nice monthly "salary" assuming what you bring will sell. First time I brought clothes in, I made $40 a month later for three sold items. That amount wasn't even for everything. Had I sold it all in a month I would have come home with about $75!

Keeping Cool On-the-Cheap

Keep your blinds closed to keep the sun out. This helps a lot!

Dehumidifiers are GREAT, if you live in a place where it's humid. I find they can be expensive on electricity, but run them when you're home and you need it most.

Ceiling fans are great for bedrooms. Invest in one and install it. They work better than other fans in my opinion and are much quieter. Fans can be SO noisy, and it's hard to sleep when they're on! I've bought one for $15 once. They aren't too expensive.

Stay hydrated! Drink lots of cold ice water! Also, make some sun tea/iced tea. Just soak 8 tea bags in about 2–3 cups of water and let sit in the sun all day. Strain. Add sugar and lemon juice to tea. Add about 4 more cups of cold water and refrigerate. YUM! Nothing like a fresh iced tea to keep you cool!

Keeping the Animals Safe

Remember that if it is **VERY, VERY HOT** outside, leave your animals at home. Don't take them with you, but if you have to, PLEASE crack the window in your car or have some water on hand to give them and leave it in the car for them to drink while you are running your errands. When I am home and it's particularly warm in the house, I place a frozen ice pack (used for lunchboxes/coolers) at the bottom of a large bowl and fill it with water for my cats. This will keep the water cool for a while—they love it!

Gardening (For People Who Kill Things)

Okay, I've taken a stab at gardening for three years now. I haven't killed anything per se, but some stuff just hasn't grown for me. I can't say I love gardening, but I love the idea of eating stuff out of my garden. Last year I would pick beans out of the garden right before dinner. It was so exhilarating!

For me, a city girl, watching stuff grow is just a miracle. I know it's weird, but honestly, eating your own grown stuff is the best feeling.

I am not here to tell you how to garden like a pro because I don't know how to either. I've attempted to read books on gardening and even asked some people to assist me and give me tips. To be honest, the whole thing just seems like so much trouble. Pick the weeds, dig up the entire garden, water every day, spray homemade pesticides on (oofffff). I can't remember the other stuff because it seems so overwhelming.

I once discussed this with my partner, and he said just to plant the seeds and let nature do its thing. Let the earth take care of it all and just sit back and watch. So that's what we did last year, and that's when my lovely beans appeared!

This year, we have a bigger garden, so we're planting all kinds of seeds. I will be starting some plants indoors too.

What I suggest is to ask neighbors, friends, and family for some snippets of their plants. Grow stuff like strawberries, rhubarb, and corn, which are apparently so easy to grow!! Just dig up some dirt and chuck the seeds in the ground and wait.

If things are growing for you, you'll get more excited, and you may eventually want to know more about it, but if you're just interested in growing your own stuff without all the headaches, just plant the seeds!!

With tomatoes, the only thing I noticed is that you need lots of SUN! It's best to plant tomato plants in a huge pot so you can move it to where the sun is. Planting from seeds is challenging so try to buy a small plant at a decent garden place. I found this works best. Plant green beans too, they're so easy! Don't be afraid to ask the garden shop in your area for a list of plants you can't possibly kill. Again, stuff like rhubarb, oregano, and mint grow like weeds, so try that first!

Another thing you can do is join a community garden. I've talked to some people who actually got into gardening because they did this. We have one in our neighborhood, but we have a big enough yard to grow our own stuff so I haven't used it myself. The community gardens are for people who can't garden where they live, so they are awesome for people who live in apartments. People also share gardening tips and will help you with your piece of the garden. This can be a cool way to meet people too!

So, go, what are you waiting for?

Frugal, Cheap, and Green Ideas for Seed Planters

Here are two ways you can make your own or reuse some containers for your seedlings:

Plastic Yogurt Containers

I acquired these at work so I decided that I will use them for planting seeds. Just drill 3 holes at the bottom of each container.

Egg Cartons or Egg Shells

Obviously, I don't eat eggs but my partner does. (The organic grain-fed free-range ones of course!) These are awesome for seedlings because you can cut the carton and plant it right in the soil when ready, same goes for the shells. If you've ever carefully cracked your egg right in half, each piece can be used to plant seeds.

I am starting to grow my own luffa this year. (Yes, it IS a vegetable!!) Apparently they are easy and bugs don't like them either. I acquired 140 seeds for $4. The guy even sent me a sample luffa and some great castor instructions. I make my own soa,p which is why I want to grow luffa. This would be a cool gift for friends/family. Luffa can be eaten when young,but I am not planning to use them for food.

Happy planting!

Vegan Traveling Tips

Traveling is fun. Traveling can also be WAY too pricey. That's why most of us are trapped where we live, with nowhere to go because time and/or money is an issue. We're stuck in our jobs working for capitalists for minimum wage. If we're lucky, we get a one-week paid vacation. So, what do we do? How can we get out of our rut and travel for little or no money?

First of all, you will need to find a little time. A week is good, although a few days is fine if you're not going too far. Here is how you can save money with transportation, accommodation, food, and entertainment while you're away. A lot of these are really obvious to me, and most of you might know these things already. Here goes . . .

Transportation

Greyhound has wicked bus passes so check these out: www.greyhound.com.

VIA Rail (Canada) or Amtrak (US) offer great passes for travel. Check out their websites for deals. I know that with VIA, if you reserve a few weeks in advance, it's cheaper.

Rideshares, though not all cities have these. However, there are companies that hook up drivers with passengers. I used these services a lot overseas. Ask around where you live. Another idea is to post an ad at universities and colleges. Some students have cars and need to drive home once in a while and will usually take other passengers to share gas/driving expenses. Also post at youth hostels for a ride! Check out Craigslist as well.

Flying is tricky. Airfares go up and down, and it's hard to predict prices in advance. If I have a set date in mind, I usually end up looking at ALL the big internet travel sites for the best deal on a flight. Once I find one, I print it out, go to my local Flight Centre (they have offices in North America and Australia) and ask them to beat the price. They always do it, even if it's by $5 a person. I may have only saved $10 more, but that's food money!

Accomodations

Ask everyone you know if they know anyone where you're going.

If you're traveling by car, sleep in your car and wash in bathrooms around town. Fancy hotels are always a good spot to get cleaned up . . . as long as you don't look suspicious or they'll throw you out.

If you have a little money, stay at a local youth hostel (anywhere from $10 to $25 a night for a bed depending on what city you're in). Some places include breakfasts, internet, and other cheap stuff. It's a good way to meet others from different countries/cities. Make friends there and visit them so you can stay there for free.

Sleep under a tree! If you're brave, find a local park that is quiet in a decent neighborhood. I probably wouldn't do this myself, but I know people who have.

Bring a tent and camp. Depending on where you wanna camp, you can pay to go to campsite (usually $10 to $20) or just in the woods somewhere if you're going to be in the country.

Free Accommodations Anywhere in the World: Couchsurfing

Try Couchsurfing.com. The BEST way to meet awesome people and get free accommodation, and if you are really lucky, your own personal tour guide. I always say that Couchsurfing.com is set up like Ebay but for travelers, and it's free. If someone crashes at your place and for whatever reason something bad happens (never experienced this personally), you can give someone a bad rating so basically no one will host them again. I've never seen bad ratings because people don't wanna get bad reviews. Be polite and be a good guest, and your host will love you and give you raving reviews, which will make others want to host you.

So far, I have only hosted people and have had really great experiences! I found that most guests like to "earn their keep," though personally, I don't expect anything because I love meeting new people. I've had people bring me gifts, cook dinner, and even wash all the sheets and towels they used before leaving. For the most part, I loved the fact that I met new people of all ages and backgrounds. It's important to fill your profile as detailed as possible because it gives people an idea of what to expect. If your house is queer friendly, say so! Pets? Smoking? (Of any kind . . . or not?)

I mention in my profile that there is full use of my kitchen but vegetarian only, just so meat eaters know they can't have a big pig roast at my house. Hehe. If you don't have a couch but can offer floor space (with or without blankets), that works too, just mention it. You can even just be available to meet people for coffee or to show them around if you don't have any space to host anyone.

The site is pretty much set up for anyone; it's fantastic. If you have a detailed profile, people know what to expect when they get there—no surprises. :) If you are a big party/drinking person, say so as well; that way you'll have guests on the same page, and you'll have a blast!

Food

Visit the local Food Not Bombs and go to their servings! Big cities have them almost every day in the evening, which means free dinners every night! Check online for local chapters.

If you can't find one there, there still might be one. Sometimes the listings on this site are outdated, and new FNB chapters are always surfacing. If you can't find it on the site, do research on the net, or when you get there, ask a cute punk kid or girl.

Eating out is expensive. Go to the local grocery store and buy foods discounted or on sale, preferably. Local dollar stores also carry cheap foods. If you have access to a kitchen (like in a hostel), then you're in luck. There are usually spices and condiments left behind from other travelers, so all you need is a few ingredients, and you can cook up a great meal!

If you MUST eat out, ask locals for cheap joints to eat at. Before traveling anywhere, I usually do a bit of research on the net to find out cheap places to dine. Try to avoid capitalist chain restaurants (insert big bad corporation names here) and dine at locally owned places. Fast food sucks anyway. Myself, I love "Mom and Pop" operations. The food is usually good if the owners are cooking!

The key here is to research the place beforehand if you can. I know a place in Montreal that serves $2 vegan meals every Thursday at one of the universities. Colleges and universities are a good place to start. Students are poor, so they need cheap food too. Again, don't be shy and ask around!

Entertainment

If you are interested in museums, most cities have a day where it's free or certain times where it's free or cheaper to get in. Ask!

Some cities have free walking tours. You can type in FREE WALKING TOURS in Google. So if you do research, you're set!

It's difficult to write more on this because each city/town is different and has different free things and activities. If you are really on a budget, do your research. Go to the library. Consult cool travel guides for info. Try the *Let's Go, Rough Guide* or *Lonely Planet* series. Stay away from *Frommer's* and *Fodor's*. I find those books are for people who have a lot more money to spend.

We have a zine archive in our town, and someone made a zine about anti-tourist places to go in our town. I, myself, have also made a four-page zine for my couchsurfers and to give to backpackers when they are visiting. I give mine away for free, so check local zine places for information too. They can be a FOUNTAIN of information. Personally, I rarely rely on traditional tourist guides that are put out by the state/province as they are geared for people who have more money than I do.

Promoting Veganism

Coolest Restaurant: Spirite Lounge in Montreal, Quebec

I was recently visiting my hometown and stumbled upon a fab restaurant: the Spirite Lounge is an organic vegetarian/vegan restaurant, and I promise you that it is unlike any other place you've ever been! The kitsch decorations give the place a wonderful feel: there is industrial aluminum foil covering most of the walls and ceilings, dim orange lighting and leopard or tiger patterned tablecloths. Entering this establishment is like embarking on a new journey.

The waitress came over, enthusiastically explaining the evening's menu. I have never seen a server so excited about food. After listing each dish, she was able to list ALL the ingredients in it with temptress sparkles in her eyes.

Okay, this is the deal at this restaurant. There is NO menu to look at. You eat what's being cooked or you're out of luck. You MUST eat every crumb on your plate or else you won't get dessert. (You think I'm kidding, don't you?) And on top of that you have to pay $2 to them. (So you know the $2 that is collected from all those sinning food wasters is saved up all year, and the restaurant matches what they've earned from the customers. The money goes to a different charity every year.) Trust me though, after you the speech you get about how you have to finish your plate, you feel like a little kid again being scolded by your mom!

Their belief is that food waste is a crime against humanity, and that no one should throw anything out. Also, if you make it to dessert but don't finish it, you're banned from the restaurant for life. (Yikes!) I am told that this rarely happens. Hey, who can't finish dessert anyway?

The good news is that they have three different portions: Regular, Reduced, or Kids size. Also remember to mention your food allergies just in case!

I warn you, this is an expensive joint but well worth the cash if you can spare it. I spent $30 on myself, and I didn't even have any wine or soup! The $30 included a reduced portion of the main entrée, an appetizer, dessert, and coffee.

I am tempted to say the food I had here is better than sex, but let's be honest here, what's really better than that? However, this was the best meal I had had in YEARS! So, on your trip to Montreal, make sure to stop in. You won't regret it!

P. S. Just so you know, I did not get anything for this review!

Organize a Vegan Potluck

This is a really fun way to get friends and family together. Ask everyone to bring a vegan dish and provide recipes for those who have no idea how to cook/bake vegan! Make sure to collect everyone's recipes and make a little booklet for everyone to use. I find that once meat eaters taste vegan dishes, they are surprised at how good everything tastes and usually ask for recipes. If you're lucky, the recipes will be passed along to others too!

Write a Newsletter

Write a one-page newsletter explaining why you are vegan, and perhaps an article or two on animal rights. Add a recipe and some website addresses so people can get further information. You can make a few hundred copies and leave them at local places: cafés, restaurants, libraries, schools, colleges, etc.

An idea might be to include your email so people can contact you about the information in your newsletter. Who knows? You might get people who want to contribute if you decide to do another one!

Organize a Vegan Info Session

If you work in a large company or go to school, you can organize a little info session about veganism. It doesn't have to be complicated and you don't have to be a big expert on all animal issues. Have a short info session about veganism and bring a few recipes for people to try out at home. Ask PETA or other animal rights organizations to provide you with a few free veggie starter kits! GoVeg.com is a good site for information!

RECIPES

Spring clean, cool off, and celebrate the warmer months with your loved ones with these delightful and practical vegan recipes rooted in the season!

DIY Cleansers and Cleaning Tips

Okay, I'll be honest, these aren't the type of cleansers that you spray on and all the dirt magically melts away. Those kinds of cleaners are full of nasty chemicals!! These homemade ones do require some extra elbow grease, but the environment will thank you. What's great is that they are inexpensive to make. (All right, they don't smell like flowers either, but feel free to add some essential oil to some of them.)

Homemade Scouring Powder

Ingredients:

- 1 cup baking soda
- 1 cup borax
- 1 cup salt

All-Purpose Disinfectant

Ingredients:

- 2 teaspoons borax
- 4 tablespoons vinegar and
- 3 to 4 cups hot water

Instructions

Pour everything into a spray bottle. For extra cleaning power, add ¼ teaspoon liquid soap to the mixture.

Toilet Bowl Cleanser

Instructions

Pour 1 cup of borax into the toilet before going to bed. In the morning, scrub and flush. For an extra-strength cleaner, add ¼ cup vinegar to the borax.

Dusting Cleanser

Instructions

Dusting is best done with a damp cloth. Dry dusting simply stirs up dust and moves it around. Try 1 teaspoon olive oil per ½ cup vinegar. Mix together in a bowl and apply with a soft cloth.

Floor Disinfectant

Instructions

Add 2 gallons of hot water to ½ cup of borax. (Put the borax in the bucket first, then add water to avoid splashing.)

Wood Floor Cleaner

Instructions

Vinegar is a natural disinfectant, and it pulls dirt from wood. After a large party, I used 1 cup vinegar per pail of hot water to clean my wood floors—the smell disappeared immediately. You can also use it on other types of floors—it's a gentle yet very effective floor cleaner.

Carpeting and Rugs

Regular vacuuming will help keep carpets their cleanest. Sprinkle baking soda over the surface of the carpet and let it stand for 15–30 minutes before vacuuming to soak up and eliminate odors.

Mold Management

If you live in an area where it's damp (like I do), you might get mold appearing in places. Honestly, the best way to get rid of it is mixing some water with bleach and spraying it on. Make sure you leave the room after doing so. I don't like using bleach but other methods I've tried don't work. I've been told you can use a baking soda/water paste and really scrub hard but this hasn't worked for me in the past. You can try it though!

Washing Shoes

People are always wondering if it's possible to wash those muddy, dirty running shoes laying around. My partner had a pair of REALLY muddy shoes (from an outside concert where it had rained). They weren't cheap shoes, so I was afraid to do anything to them. I decided to bite the bullet and throw them in the wash (on a delicate cycle) with some detergent (low water). (I'd put ¼ cup of baking soda as well, if the shoes in question were particularly stinky.) They came out spotless!

Don't put shoes in the dryer though. Air dry them. To make them dry faster, put some newspaper inside the shoe; this will soak up the water fairly quickly. Change the newspaper every hour or so, for maximum water absorbing! You can also put them in front of a small fan as well to speed it up even more.

Making/Recycling Your Own Cleaning Tools

Scrubbers: Cut up pieces of mesh potato bags and tie into a small ball—works great for scouring dishes!

Sponges: Throw your dirty sponge in the dishwasher or boil it with a bit of baking soda on the stove to make it look like new again.

Towels: Cut up old towels instead of throwing them away, and use them for dishcloths or in the garage.

Toothbrushes: Save that old toothbrush! You can use it to scrub floors, stains on clothing, and more!

Mop: To make a new mop head, try cutting up strips of old towels, shirts, or socks. Rubberband or tie the top ends of the strips together, then secure to the mop stick.

Window Cleaner: I've heard that newspaper works well to clean windows. You can also try old cloth diapers.

Getting Rid of Fruit Flies

As much as I'd love to say I love all living things, truthfully I can't stand fruit flies. They seem to attach themselves to everything. **ARGH!** Here are two methods to get rid of them:

Place a banana peel or ripe piece of fruit in a large plastic bag (I use recycled bread bags). Leave the bag open at the top and wait a few hours. Tons of the flies will go in there, then quickly close the bag and throw it out or let the flies loose far away from your house! You can also use an empty jar doing the same thing. Another way is to place vinegar or wine in a glass or bowl, cover with plastic wrap and poke with tiny holes using a toothpick or needle. They'll be able to fly in there but not get out.

Another way to get rid of them is hope that you have a resident hungry spider like I do! A very cute spider made a web above my sink and has been trapping and eating any fruit flies remaining in my kitchen. I've watched her move, she's fast! Go spidey!

Beauty, Skin Care, and Remedies

Summer is a great time to take care of your whole body. Enjoy these recipes for the care and keeping of yourself and others during spring and summer.

Hair Buildup Remover

Ingredients:

- ¼ cup vinegar
- 1 cup water

Instructions:
After conditioning the hair, use this as a final rinse. Leaves your hair soft and shiny.

Hair Conditioner

Instructions:
Combine mashed avocado with some coconut milk. Comb it through the hair and let sit for 10 to 15 minutes, rinse out.

Easy Foot Scrub

Ingredients:

- ¼ cup fine sea salt
- 2 tablespoon sweet almond, olive, or grapeseed oil
- 1 teaspoon of castile soap
- 6–8 drops of tea tree or peppermint essential oil (you can use geranium for bad circulation)

- 1 vitamin E capsule (optional: use only if you will store the mixture for a while)

Instructions:
Mix everything in a bowl and store in a container that is not see-through (or one that is very dark, like an amber glass/plastic jar). To use, just scrub on feet, rinse, and pat dry. Apply lotion afterwards. NOTE: If you do not add the vitamin E, the oil will go rancid quickly. If you do not have vitamin E, just store the mixture in the fridge.

Facial Exfoliator Recipe

Ingredients:

- 2 heaped teaspoons fine oatmeal
- 1 teaspoon baking soda

Instructions:
Combine ingredients, and add enough water to make a paste. Apply to skin and rub gently. Rinse and gently pat dry.

Oatmeal Bath

Instructions:
Don't buy those expensive packages of oatmeal bath powder—you can make your own! Blend one cup of oatmeal (instant, unflavored oatmeal, quick oats, or slow-cooking oats—doesn't matter which kind) in a food processor, blender, or well-cleaned coffee grinder. Process the oats until fine. Add about ½ cup of the processed oats to the warm running water of your bath, and swirl to spread the oats and create a silky, milky bath. Your skin will thank you!

Citrus Hair Spray

Instructions:

Chop 1 lemon (or orange for dry hair). Place in a pot with 2 cups of water, and boil until only half of the original amount remains. Cool, strain, and place in a spray bottle.

Easy Lip Balm

Ingredients:

- 2 tablespoons sweet almond oil
- 2 tablespoons coconut oil (I used the organic stuff I cook with.)
- 1 tablespoons melted beeswax (non-bee alternative: carnauba wax)
- 2 vitamin E capsules
- 8 drops peppermint or sweet orange essential oil

Instructions:

For containers, not tubes. Melt everything (aside from vitamin E) in the microwave on medium heat for a minute. Stir, check after every minute, and stir; you don't want it to get too hot. Once *just melted*, stir in the vitamin E and essential oils and pour into small containers. This didn't take long to harden as the oil wasn't too hot. I made some labels on my laser printer and covered the labels with a piece of tape to prevent wear and tear. *If you want to use lip balm tubes instead of containers, add more beeswax—probably 50% more—as you want a harder consistency.*

Other container ideas: empty film canisters (go to Walmart to get them, they have tons to give away), pill boxes or containers, contact lens cases (1 of each flap)

Cucumber Sunburn Lotion

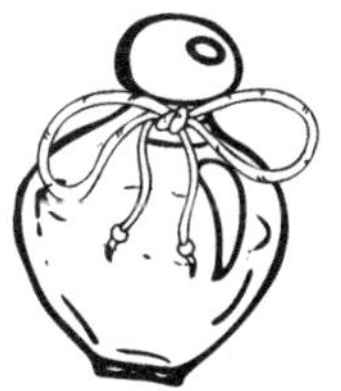

Ingredients:

- 1 cucumber, chopped
- ¼ cup glycerin
- ¼ cup rosewater

Instructions:

Squeeze juice out of the cucumber with a lemon squeezer and mix with glycerin and rosewater.

Sunburn Mist

Ingredients:

- 2 fluid ounces of distilled water
- 9 drops of lavender
- 2 drops of peppermint
- 1 drop of spearmint

Instructions:

Mix all, then mist lightly over sunburned skin.

Itchy Bites Salve

There are so many black flies where we live. They always get me; this will stop the itch!

Ingredients:

- 2 tablespoons dried chickweed
- 2 tablespoons dried plantain leaves
- 1 tablespoon dried yarrow
- 1 cup olive oil

Instructions:

Infuse oil/herbs on the lowest heat possible. Let sit for at least an hour. Strain, then pour oil back into pot and add some beeswax (1 ounce or so). When beeswax is melted, pour into tiny glass jars.

Cooking Substitutes

Sometimes we don't have all the ingredients on hand when we want to cook something, or we realize halfway through the recipe that we don't have a specific ingredient! What now?? Here are some fabulous substitutions!

Mock Buttermilk

Place 1 tablespoon of lemon juice or white vinegar (vinegar makes a whiter product) in a standard measuring cup. Fill to the 1 cup mark with soy milk.

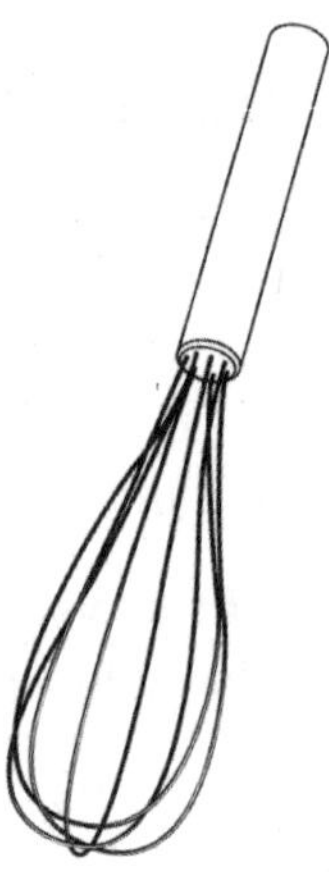

Brown Sugar

One cup firmly packed brown sugar equals 1 cup granulated sugar plus 1 tablespoon of molasses.

Baking Powder

One teaspoon of baking powder equals ¼ teaspoon of baking soda plus 3/8 teaspoon cream of tartar.

Cake Flour

If your recipe calls for cake flour and all you have is all-purpose flour, here is what you can do: Add 1 tablespoon of cornstarch to a 1 cup measuring cup. Add all-purpose flour till you have 1 cup of mixture. This is equivalent to a cup of cake flour.

Self-Rising Flour

1 ½ teaspoon baking powder and ½ teaspoon salt in a measuring cup, adding all-purpose flour to equal 1 cup.

Thick White Icing

- 4 cups icing sugar
- 1 cup shortening
- 5 tablespoons water
- 1 tablespoon artificial vanilla extract (you can use other flavorings as well, but just use 1 teaspoon)

Instructions:

Blend all ingredients with a hand blender and whip till it becomes a nice smooth thick icing. This isn't too sweet and is great for icing all sorts of cakes. You can experiment with different colors and flavors. Use less water if you want to use this to decorate.

Nut and Seed Milks

There are so many milk variations! They are all easy to make. I didn't include rice milk because of the carbohydrates. I read that there aren't too many vitamins in rice milk, so stick to nut or seed milks (or soy) if you can. It's also better to make these yourself as there are no chemicals in there. These are best consumed within 4 days or so if possible. Because they are easy to make you can whip them up frequently.

Cashew Milk

It was late at night, and I realized I wanted to make bread first thing in the morning, but I didn't have any non-dairy milk on hand;. All I had was some raw cashews to make nut milk. Here is what I came up with:

Take about 1 ½ cups of cashews and soak them overnight if you can. Strain them, then add about 4 to 5 cups of water and nuts in a blender and blend until smooth, then strain. Add a few pinches of salt and 1 tablespoon sweetener if you wish. Great to use for anything!

Almond Milk
Bought tons of raw almonds and did the same thing as with the cashew milk.

Sunflower Seed Milk
Though a bit fattier than other milks, this is easy to make. No need to pre-soak seeds but if you have the time you can soak them for 3-4 hours beforehand. Use about ½ cup sunflower seeds to 1 ½ cups of water.

Other nuts, seeds to use: pecans, pine nuts, walnuts, pumpkin seeds, sesame seeds. I find it always nicer to pre-soak if possible.

Spring/Summer Cool-down Treats

Lemon-Lime Ginger Ice

Ingredients:

- 1 cup water
- 1 cup sugar
- ½ cup lemon juice
- ⅓ cup lime juice
- 1 tablespoon freshly grated ginger
- 1 teaspoon each of lemon and lime rind (optional)

Frozen Gourmet Chocolate Chip Cookie Dough

If you love the taste of freshly baked cookies right out of the oven but can't handle the burden of making them all the time, here's a great solution: Make your own cookie dough and freeze it! This way, you can make any amount of cookies you want. I hear you can freeze for about 2 months but have seen other articles where they have frozen it up to 6 months. This would also be a great gift for a friend or family member who doesn't like to bake but loves homemade goods.

Ingredients:

- 1 cup margarine, softened
- 1 cup white sugar
- 1 cup packed brown sugar
- equivalent to 2 egg replacers
- 2 teaspoons vanilla extract
- 3 cups all-purpose flour
- 1 teaspoon baking soda
- 2 teaspoons hot water
- ½ teaspoon salt
- 2 cups semisweet chocolate chips
- 1 cup chopped walnuts

Instructions:

Cream together the margarine, white sugar, and brown sugar until smooth. Add the egg replacer and vanilla. Dissolve baking soda in hot water. Add to batter, along with salt. Stir in flour, chocolate chips, and nuts.

If you are going to freeze this, roll it into a log and wrap it in plastic wrap. Then, place in a large ziplock bag or wrap again tightly with aluminum foil. Remember to label it. You can also store this in a shallow plastic container and cover with plastic wrap. This makes it easier to scoop the dough frozen and place right on the cookie sheet.

Some sites say to defrost the dough before baking it, but I've sliced it and baked it as is while frozen with no problems!

To Bake:

Drop by large spoonfuls or slice dough and place onto ungreased pans. Bake for about 10 minutes in a 350°F preheated oven, or until edges are browned.

Really Cool Rainbow Popsicles

Don't eat those cruddy sugar-water popsicles. Make these!!

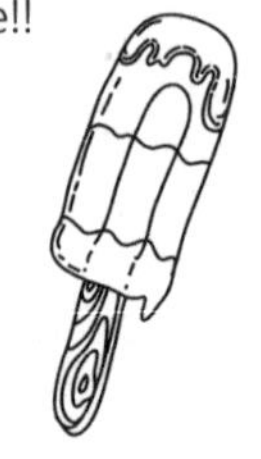

Ingredients:

- pineapple juice
- cranberry juice
- orange juice

Instructions

Use a popsicle mold and pour ⅓ of any type of juice. Freeze. Repeat until you have three layers. This takes a bit but is worth it and tastes so much better than store-bought junk.

Orange Sorbet

Ingredients:

- 2 cups fresh orange juice
- 2 tablespoons lemon juice
- 1 cup water
- 1 cup sugar

Instructions:

Heat 1 cup of water and the sugar in a saucepan until dissolved. Bring to a boil, simmer for 2 minutes, and leave to cool.

Stir the orange juice and lemon juice into the sugar syrup. Chill the mixture. Freeze the mixture in an ice cream machine, using it according to the manufacturer's instruction.

Instructions:

Put water and sugar in a small saucepan. Bring mixture to a boil, then let simmer for 1 to 2 minutes.

Cool (I place this in the fridge so it cools faster).

Once the mixture is cooled, pour it into a blender with all other ingredients and blend till smooth.

Strain the mixture through a fine sieve. Pour it into an ice cream maker and follow the manufacturer's instructions.

Piña Colada Sorbet

Ingredients:

- 2 cups crushed pineapple
- ½ cup cream of coconut
- ⅓ cup granulated sugar
- ⅓ cup water
- ¼ cup dark rum

Instructions:

Place undrained pineapple and cream of coconut in a large container.

Combine sugar and water.

Bring to a boil over medium heat and boil for 1 minute. Cool.

Add sugar syrup and rum to the pineapple mixture.

Freeze until firm, about 4 to 6 hours.

Process in a blender or food processor until smooth but not completely thawed.

Freeze until firm.

Soften lightly before serving.

Chocolate-Coffee Sorbet

Ingredients:

- 2 cups water
- ⅔ cup sugar
- 5 ounces dark chocolate (70% cocoa)
- 1 tablespoon coffee grounds

Instructions:

In a pot, pour 1.5 cups of water, the sugar, and the cocoa powder.

Bring to a boil, and let simmer for 5 minutes. Add the chocolate (cut up in small chunks). Bring to a boil again, stirring constantly, then immediately remove the pot from the heat. Let the mixture cool down quickly (ideally, put the pot in cold water and stir until cool).

With the ½ cup remaining water and the coffee grounds, make some coffee.

Let the coffee cool down and add it to the chocolate mixture.

When everything is completely cooled down, pour in your favorite ice cream maker, and voilà, chocolate-coffee sorbet!

Grapefruit Mint Sorbet

Yummy and refreshing, good palate cleanser. Also perfect for those super hot days.

Ingredients:

- 1 to ½ cups sugar
- 1 cup water
- ½ cup fresh mint leaves, chopped very fine
- ⅓ cups fresh ruby red or pink grapefruit juice, strained

Instructions:

Stir the sugar, mint, and water together in a saucepan. Place over low heat and stir until the sugar is dissolved.

Increase heat to medium-high and boil for 30 seconds without stirring.

Remove from heat, pour into a heatproof bowl, and cool completely.

Pour the grapefruit juice into a large bowl and stir in 1 cup of the syrup. Taste and add 1 to 3 tablespoons of more syrup, if needed. Cover and place in the freezer.

When well chilled, transfer to an ice cream machine and process according to the manufacturer's directions. Cover tightly and freeze until ready to serve.

Green Tea Sorbet

Strapped for cash and need a quick dessert for a potluck or need something sweet for yourself? This makes LOTS and costs pennies to make. I've made it with flavored green tea because that's all I had. I also used dark rum.

Ingredients:

- 3 cups strong green tea (but any kind of tea will do)
- 3 cups sugar
- Splash of rum or other sweet liqueur

Instructions:

The tea should be drinkable, but strong. The mixture will taste too sweet but the flavors will mellow with freezing. Pour into ice cream maker and proceed according to directions.

Strawberry Sorbet

Ingredients:

- 5 cups strawberries
- ⅔ cups sugar
- ⅔ cups water
- 2 tablespoons lemon juice

Basic Bean Burgers

Ingredients:

- 1 cup TVP granules (textured vegetable protein)
- 1 cup boiling water
- 1 tablespoon tomato paste or ketchup
- 16-ounce can pinto, kidney, or other beans, drained
- ¼ cup whole wheat breadcrumbs
- 2 cloves garlic, finely minced
- ½ teaspoon oregano
- 1 tablespoon tamari or soy sauce
- 1 teaspoon sweetener
- salt and pepper to taste
- whole wheat flour for dusting

Pour boiling water over TVP and tomato paste in a bowl. Stir and let rest for 10 minutes. In a food processor, combine TVP mixture and remaining ingredients except for flour. Pulse until mixture is almost a puree. Dust hands with flour and shape mixture into 6 burgers. Dust them lightly in flour. Layer the burgers with sheets of waxed paper and refrigerate for at least 1 hour. Cook on a grill covered with foil for about 10 minutes on each side.

Beet This Burger

Ingredients:

- 1 tablespoon finely grated raw beet
- ½ cup cooked oats (quick or regular rolled oats)
- 1 cup uncooked oats (quick or regular rolled oats)
- ½ cup walnuts, coarsely ground
- ¼ cup almonds, coarsely ground
- 2 tablespoons sesame seeds
- 1 tablespoon instant vegetable broth
- ¼ cup green pepper, minced
- ¼ cup celery, minced
- ¼ cup onion, minced
- 1 teaspoon dried basil
- ¼ teaspoon dried thyme
- ¼ teaspoon dried thyme
- ¼ teaspoon ground sage
- ¼ teaspoon mustard powder
- 2 tablespoons soy sauce
- 1 tablespoon nutritional yeast flakes (optional)

Instructions:

Mix all ingredients together well. Form into patties and grill until cooked through. Serve on whole wheat rolls with tomato slices and your favorite condiments.

TVP Sweet Potato Burgers with Maple Carrots

Soak ½ cup TVP granules in ½ cup boiling water for 5 minutes.

Transfer to a large bowl. Peel and cube the sweet potato, then cook in boiling water till tender. Mash and let cool a little. Add to TVP, then add ¼ cup breadcrumbs (make this in a food processor using the purchased bread roll), some salt and pepper and 1 teaspoon crushed rosemary to taste and stir well.

Form 4 patties and refrigerate for an hour if you have time. Fry up for a few minutes on both sides till warmed up.

Cut up as many carrots as you need and boil for about 5 minutes till tender. Drain and add a little oil or butter and some pure maple syrup or brown sugar if you have it on hand.

Curry Tofu Burgers

A little one of my inventions that turned out! Woohoo!

Ingredients:

- 1 pour frozen block of tofu thawed out (squeeze excess water too)
- 2 cups warm water
- 1 tablespoon curry powder
- 1 teaspoon salt
- 1 teaspoon hot sauce or chili flakes
- ¼ teaspoon cumin

Instructions:

Cut tofu block in half, then cut each half into threes. This will give you 6 square-ish burgers. In a rectangle container, add all ingredients, mix, then add tofu. Marinate for over an hour, overnight if you can. Then fry a few minutes on each side till browned. Serve on small dinner buns with condiments.

Sidewalk Café Paninis

Paninis are SO good, but obviously I don't have one of those fancy grills they use at the cafes to make them. Here is how you can make a mouthwatering panini at home! (Thanks for this idea, Mikkel!!)

Ingredients:

- 2 buns (oblong, perhaps 6-inch ones)
- red pepper slices
- vegan sliced cheeze (mozza style)
- olives
- any other toppings you want

Instructions:

Place the ingredients between the buns. Oil top and bottom with olive oil. Wrap 1 brick with a piece of foil. Place buns in a pan on medium heat (if you have one with grill ridges even better). Place brick on top of the 2 buns and grill a few minutes, turn over, place the brick on again and grill the other side. Voila! YUM!

Curried Lentil Stew

Instructions:

In a saucepan, fry up 1 onion in a little oil, then add 1 teaspoon salt, 2 teaspoons curry powder, and some pepper. Cook until onion becomes translucent. Add lentils, a can of diced tomatoes, then fill the empty can with water and add to saucepan. Bring to a boil, then simmer for 30 minutes until lentils are tender. I usually puree this with a hand blender. (You can add one diced carrot to this too if you want!) I had a few small dumpstered ones on hand that I added in there. I also usually add some red chili flakes or hot sauce for a kick. Serve with salvaged bread if you have it.

Graeme's Luscious Lentil Soup

This is such an easy recipe and quite filling. Feeds lots of people! This can also easily be frozen in portions to use for lunches or dinners.

Ingredients:

- 2 to 3 onions, chopped
- garlic (as much as you'd like), chopped
- 6 to 8 potatoes, cubed
- 2 cups red lentils
- vegetable stock (powder or concentrate)
- a few dashes each of cumin, coriander, curry power, salt pepper, and olive oil

Instructions:

Saute onions and garlic in the olive oil over low-medium heat until onions are transparent.

Add 8 to 10 cups of water and bring to boil.

Add stock, spices, and potatoes.

Bring back to boil.

Add lentils.

Simmer on low until lentils are cooked.

Potato, Black Bean, and Corn Stew

At the end of the summer, we're blessed with lots of corn and some new potatoes! Here is what you can make—feeds an army of folks.

Ingredients:

- 2 onions, chopped
- 4 cups of fresh corn (about 4 to 6 ears—just cut off the kernels)
- 5 potatoes, diced
- 19-ounce can of black beans, drained and rinsed
- 8 cups veggie stock
- 1 teaspoon cumin

- ½ teaspoon paprika
- 1 teaspoon salt
- ¼ teaspoon pepper

Instructions:

Fry onions in a little oil for about a minute. Add all other ingredients and bring to a boil. Then turn down heat and simmer on medium-low until potatoes are cooked. Use hand blender to blend part of the stew. You can blend it all, but I like leaving some chunks in there!

Spicy Summer Squash and Potato Soup

I ended up with way too many yellow squash this year; here's a soup that was created because of this.

Ingredients:

- 1 onion, diced
- 2 garlic cloves, minced
- 1 large yellow squash—peeled, seeded, and cubed
- 3 potatoes
- 3 cups water or veggie stock
- 1 teaspoon salt
- 1 teaspoon curry powder
- ¼ teaspoon turmeric
- a few pinches of cinnamon
- 1 teaspoon chili sauce, red pepper flakes, or sambal

Instructions:

Fry up onion and cloves in a little oil for a minute. Add all other ingredients and cook on medium-low heat until potatoes and squash are tender. Use a hand blender to blend soup. Serve with fresh bread or crackers.

Broccoli and Red Pepper Salad

Ingredients:

- 3 cups broccoli florets
- 1 medium red pepper, diced
- 1 tablespoon sesame oil
- 1 garlic clove, minced
- 1 lemon peel (maybe 1 tablespoon)
- 1 tablespoon fresh lemon juice
- ¼ teaspoon salt
- ⅛ teaspoon red pepper flakes

Cook broccoli for about 3 minutes, then cool. Heat sesame oil in a pan and fry garlic for a minute. Add all ingredients in a bowl and refrigerate. Serve cold.

Raspberry Cucumber Tomato Salad

I made raspberry vinegar with berries in my yard and had cucumbers and tomatoes from my garden. Here's what I came up with:

Salad:

- 1 large cucumber, diced
- 1 large tomato, seeded and diced
- ¼ cup Spanish onion, diced

Dressing:

- 2 tablespoons raspberry vinegar (or other fruit vinegar)
- 2 tablespoons oil (any kind but canola is nice)
- a few pinches of dill weed (or 1 tablespoon fresh dill)

Ingredients:

Combine salad ingredients in a bowl and stir. Shake dressing ingredients in a jar and pour on salad. Eat!

Jake's Lemon Pepper Pasta

Ingredients:

- 2 cups dry pasta
- 2 to 3 cloves garlic, minced
- ½ teaspoon red pepper flakes
- lemon juice from 1 lemon
- lots of pepper
- salt to taste
- ½ pound tofu, chopped in cubes

Instructions:

Fry tofu in a little oil with garlic and red pepper flakes. Add lemon juice and pepper to tofu till browned. When pasta is done, drain it, and put in olive oil. Cover with more pepper and lemon juice. Stir in tofu. Add salt and pepper to taste. Vegan parmesan cheese can be added.

Pesto Pasta

Pesto:

- 3 garlic cloves
- ⅓ cup walnuts
- 3 cups fresh basil leaves, packed
- ½ teaspoon salt
- ¼ teaspoon pepper
- ½ cup olive oil

Instructions:

Place the garlic and nuts in a food processor and process till minced. Add basil, salt, and pepper, then ground into a paste. While the machine is running, pour the oil into the feed tube slowly in a steady stream until well blended. Stir in soy cheese, cover, and refrigerate. Cook 2 cups of dried pasta according to package directions, then add enough pesto so it becomes nice and creamy. (Maybe ¼ cup?) Enjoy!

Tomato-y Ramen Noodle

I realize that Ramen Noodles are not high up there on the "good food for you" list, but let's face it, they do come in handy when you're really broke and hungry. Like regular noodles, they are versatile and filling. Here's one of my concoctions, though I'm sure someone else has thought of it before!

Ingredients:

- 1 package of ramen noodles (discard the sketchy MSG flavor pouch!)
- ¼ cup canned tomato soup (not diluted)
- salt and pepper
- ¼ cup of veggies (your choice)

Instructions:

Boil water and start to cook the veggies first if they take longer than the noodles. After a few minutes, throw in the noodles and cook for 3 minutes. Strain and add soup, then salt and pepper to taste. Mix and eat. Are you full now?

Frugal Black Beans and Polenta

Ingredients:

- 6 cups water
- 2 cups cornmeal
- ½ teaspoon sea salt
- 2 15-ounce cans of black beans, drained and rinsed
- ½ cup salsa

Instructions:

To make polenta, bring the water and salt to a boil. Then add the cornmeal very slowly so it doesn't clump. Keep stirring on low heat until it's really thick. Be careful because it will bubble and splash! This might take 20 minutes or so. When it is thickened, and comes off the sides of the pot, spread onto a 9 x 13 greased pan. While polenta is sitting, combine black beans and salsa in sauce pan on medium heat. When polenta is cooled a bit (10 minutes or so), cut into 12 even pieces. Place 2 pieces of polenta on a plate and scoop some black bean mixture on top. This is really filling and tasty! Feel free to add other veggies if you like.

Very Lazy Quickie Veggie Paté

This is a no-nonsense paté and doesn't make too much. It was something I made when I wanted paté but didn't have most of the ingredients.

Ingredients:

- ½ cup sunflower seeds
- ½ cup water
- ⅛ cup oil
- 1 small onion (coarsely chopped)
- 1 garlic clove
- ½ teaspoon salt
- 1 teaspoon oregano
- 2 teaspoon soy sauce or Braggs
- 2 tablespoons flour

Instructions:

Throw everything into a food processor and blend till smooth. Pour into a mini loaf pan (or small baking pan) and bake for 40 minutes at 350°F. Good served warm on crackers!

Gingered Chickpeas and Rice

Instructions:

Soak 1 cup chickpeas in 5 cups of water overnight. Then cook with 4 cups of water until ready, which will be about 1 ½ hours. You can actually prepare these ahead of time and keep them in the fridge with water until ready to use. Cut up 1 onion, mince a 2-inch piece of ginger (should give you about 2 tablespoons of ginger), and fry in a little oil for about a minute. In a bowl, add a veggie broth cube and 3 cups of water and mix till dissolved. Mix 2 tablespoons of cornstarch or flour with a few tablespoons of water, then add to veggie broth. Pour this in with the onions and add the chickpeas. Cook on medium heat until thick. Season with salt and pepper if needed. Cook up the rice. Put chickpeas on top of rice and eat with friends!

Korean Fried Rice

There's a Korean restaurant near where I live, and they serve the best veggie rice. Looked pretty simple, so I created something that tastes very similar. Doesn't look like much but it's extremely flavorful!

Ingredients:

- 1 cup rice
- 2 tablespoons toasted sesame oil (replacing it with another oil will change the taste)
- 1 teaspoon Korean hot chili sauce (or hot sauce, sambal oelek, etc.)
- 2 cups veggies (broccoli, carrots, beans, bean sprouts, etc.)
- 1 small onion
- 1 very large garlic clove (or a couple of small ones)
- salt and pepper to taste

Instructions:
Cook the rice, then place in the fridge to cool. Then, heat up the sesame oil and add your onion and garlic. Fry for a few minutes. Add veggies and cook until they are done. Add cooled rice, chili sauce, and salt and pepper to taste. Fry for a few minutes and serve.

Graeme's Grilled Vegetable Peanut Skewers

First time I had this I just about died. It's so good!

What you do is put veggies on skewers (make sure you only have one type of veggie per skewer): a whole skewer of garlic cloves, a few of onion chunks, some mushrooms, peppers, broccoli, etc.

(P. S. Also, make sure you soak the skewers on their own about an hour so they won't burn on the grill.)

To make the sauce:

- about ½ cup natural peanut butter
- ⅓ cup soy yogurt
- 1 tablespoon soy sauce
- 1 tablespoon of brown sugar

Instructions:
Mix it all and brush generously on veg grill, turning occasionally until veggi garlic take a bit longer, so put those more sauce on the veggies while the off skewers and eat!

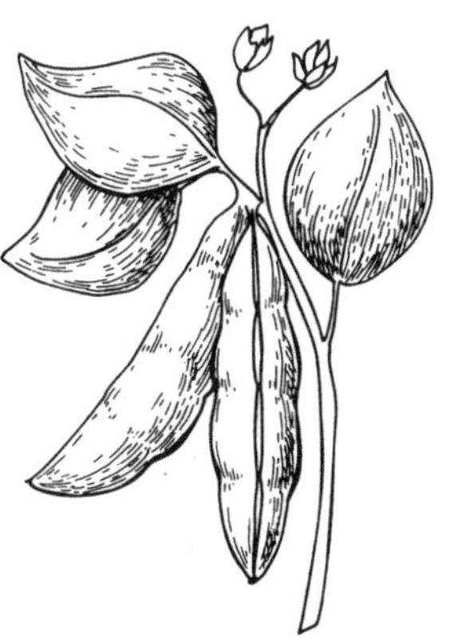

Garlic Lima Beans

I got some lima beans on sale super cheap and ended up making this one day.

Ingredients:

- 1 cup dried white lima beans (either size)
- 5 small garlic cloves (or 3 large)
- 1 onion
- 1 veggie bouillon cube
- salt and pepper to taste
- 2 cups water
- 2 tablespoons cornstarch

Instructions:

Soak lima beans overnight or for several hours. In a large pot, fry chopped onion and minced garlic in a little oil for about 1 to 2 minutes. Add water, veggie cube, and beans, then bring to a boil. Simmer on medium-low heat until beans are done. When they are done, mix some of the liquid with the cornstarch, then add to pot. Bring to a boil again and cook till thickened a bit. Season with some salt and pepper if needed. Serve on rice.

Spring/Summer Sauces, Jams, and More

Ketchup au tomates vertes du Quebec (Green tomato ketchup from Quebec)

I grew up in Quebec and this is what was done with green tomatoes! Yum! Good on veggie dogs and burgers!

Ingredients:

- 8 cups of sliced green tomatoes
- 3 tablespoons of pickling salt
- 3 cups of chopped onions
- 1 ¼ cups sugar
- 1 red pepper, diced
- 2 cups of cider vinegar (I used white when I made it)
- 3 tablespoon of mustard seeds
- 1 teaspoon turmeric
- ⅛ teaspoon cayenne pepper

Instructions:

Place tomatoes in a large pot with salt and let sit overnight on the counter. Strain tomatoes when done and set aside in a bowl. In the pot, place all ingredients except onions and red pepper and boil for 5 minutes.

Add all other ingredients, bring to a boil, then simmer for 45 minutes. Pour into hot sterilized jars and put in hot water bath for 10 minutes. Enjoy!

BBQ Sauce

Ingredients:

- 2 cups vinegar
- 1 cup water
- ½ cup ketchup
- 2 ½ tablespoons chili powder
- 1 teaspoon pepper
- 1 ½ tablespoons brown sugar
- 1 tablespoon lemon juice
- ½ teaspoon salt

Instructions:

Bring vinegar and water to simmer. Add other ingredients and stir well. Store in a squeeze bottle.

Lisa's Own Uncheeze Mix

I make this and use it a lot! Makes fabulous mock macaroni and cheese.

Ingredients:

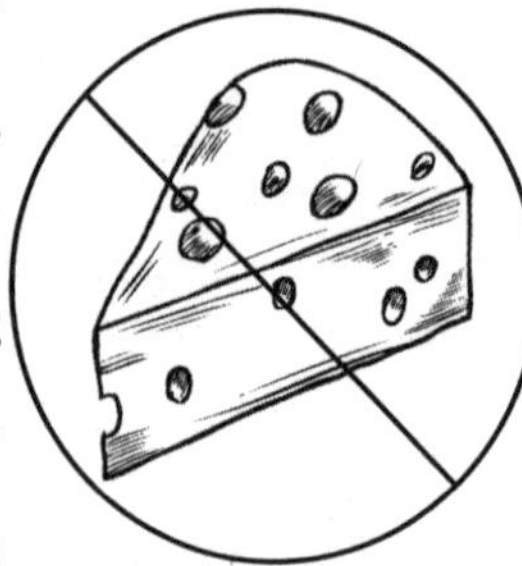

- 1 cup nutritional yeast
- 1 teaspoon garlic salt
- 1 teaspoon turmeric
- ½ teaspoon mustard powder

Instructions:

Blend all ingredients together in a small food processor or just mix by hand.

To make Mac and Cheeze:

Use ¼ cup mix for about 1 ½ to 2 cups cooked noodles, 1 teaspoon margarine, and a few tablespoons soy milk or water. Mix until nice and creamy!

Compost Vegetable Broth

I am sure a lot of you know this, but it's imperative that I write it again: Don't buy those expensive veggie broth cubes! What I do is keep a plastic container in my freezer with collected veggie scraps/peelings, herbs that are no longer super fresh, and almost un-edible veggies. After about a week, it's full. I dump it into the largest pot I have, add water to the top, and simmer on med/low for about an hour. Strain, and you have veggie broth! Freeze what you're not going to use right away.

I use this broth in my veggie casseroles, all kinds of soups and stews. I find that little veggie peelings go a long way. You can even use as little as one cup of veggie scraps, which can give you a liter or more of broth. My problem is, I end up with too many veggie scraps! I have at least 6 containers of ready-made veggie broth in the freezer.

Creamy Artichoke Dip

I want to thank BruC for inspiring this creation. 

Ingredients:

- 1 package silken tofu (12-ounce)
- 1 can artichoke hearts (15-ounce), drained
- 1 teaspoon sea salt
- ½ teaspoon dill
- ¼ cup nutritional yeast
- ¼ teaspoon pepper

Instructions:

Place all ingredients in a blender and mix until very smooth. Pour into a tight container and chill a few hours before serving. Great with veggies and rice chips!

Sweet Summer Salad Dressing

I love this stuff! It's a weird brown color but it tastes sweet and so delicious!

Ingredients:

- ¼ cup oil
- ¼ cup balsamic vinegar
- ½ tablespoon nutritional yeast
- ¼ teaspoon dried basil
- 1 tablespoon maple syrup
- 1 garlic clove, minced

Instructions:

Throw it all in a blender and blend, blend, blend! Serve over a nice salad full of greens and veggies.

Guy's Avocado Dressing

Someone made this at a potluck I went to, and I loved it! He didn't have an exact recipe, and neither do I, but it's easy to make this dish your own.

In a blender, put 1 diced avocado, some balsamic vinegar (maybe ¼ cup), about 2 teaspoons of dried dill, some salt, pepper, a few tablespoons of tamari or Braggs, and some water to make it runnier. I also use a little nutritional yeast, but that's optional! This is soooooooooooo creamy!!

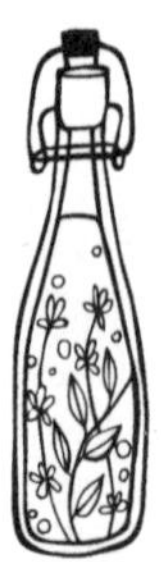

Flavored Syrups

These are popular to flavor coffee and lattes. Makes a nice gift too! Place in gift baskets with coffee!

Ingredients:

- 2 cups water
- 2 cups sugar
- your favorite flavored extracts, to taste

Instructions:

In a heavy saucepan, stir sugar and water over medium heat, until sugar is dissolved. Bring to a boil and boil for one minute. Add flavorings to taste. Pour into a pretty bottle and label. Store refrigerated. Some favorite combinations: vanilla and almond and hazelnut, vanilla, and orange.

Raspberry Vinegar

This is a great way to use up some raspberries and makes a great gift.

Ingredients:

- ½ cup raspberries
- 2 cups white vinegar

Instructions:

Put the raspberries in a 500 ml jar, then add vinegar to the top (about 2 cups). Wait 1 to 2 weeks, then strain and store in a glass bottle. You can use small wine bottles, cork it, then dip in some leftover wax to seal! Label.

Blueberry Vinegar

I like making a basket with this one and the raspberry vinegar for gifts!

Instructions:

- 1 cup blueberries (I use the small, low-bush ones)
- 2 cups white vinegar
- 2 tablespoons sugar (I use brown sugar, but any is ok!)

Instructions:

Place blueberries in a 1-quart glass jar. Add vinegar and sugar in a saucepan, cover, then bring to a boil. Take off heat and pour over berries. Let stand for 3 days, then strain and store in airtight containers or small bottles with corks. Seal with wax.

Cassis Jam (Black Currant)

This is a really easy recipe to follow no matter how many currants you have. No pectin needed!

The key is to use as much sugar as you have currants. I had 12 ounces of currants, so I used the same amount of sugar and water. I got two 250 ml jars from this plus about ¼ cup.

Place the washed currants in a saucepan and add water. Bring to boil, then reduce heat to low and simmer for 30 minutes. Add sugar, then bring back to another roaring boil, keep heat on high and boil hard for 10 minutes. Let cool for 5 minutes, then store in canning jars and close tightly. Use the hot water bath method for 5 minutes to seal jars.

Rhubarb Jam

Another favorite of mine when rhubarb is abundant! Makes a great gift too!

Ingredients:

- 5 cups chopped raw rhubarb
- 2 teaspoons orange zest
- ⅓ cup orange juice

- ½ cup water
- 2 cups sugar

Instructions:

Combine rhubarb, sugar, peel, juice and water in a heavy, non-aluminum 4-quart saucepan. Bring to a boil, reduce heat to a simmer, cover and cook gently for 45 minutes. Stir often. Remove from heat and fill hot, sterilized ½-pint jars to within ⅛-inch of the top. Wipe rims clean, attach new lids, and screw caps on tightly. Process in a boiling water bath for 10 minutes. (Note: Make only single batches. Don't try to double or triple the amount.)

Colorful Marmalade

Because of the maraschino cherries, this looks really nice in jars! Costs about $4 to make, which will give you 7 to 8 250 ml jars.

Ingredients:

- 3 oranges
- 1 lemon
- 1 grapefruit
- 2 cups crushed pineapple
- 6 cups sugar
- ½ cup chopped maraschino cherries

Instructions:

Put everything in a heavy, large saucepan except for cherries. Bring to a boil, then lower to medium-low heat and cook for 25 minutes. After 20 minutes, add cherries. Fill sterilized hot jars and process in boiling water bath for 10 minutes. Remove and let stand for 24 hours undisturbed.

No Pectin Strawberry Rhubarb Jam

Who needs pectin?! I rarely use it to make jam. Personally, I don't mind if my jam isn't as thick as the ones in the store! Making jam with fruit and a little sugar is just fine!

Right now, rhubarb and strawberries are in season. Just take about 4 cups of chopped rhubarb, 3 cups of sugar, 2 teaspoons lemon or orange zest, ¼ cup orange or lemon juice, ½ cup water and bring to a boil, then simmer for 20 minutes. Mash 2 cups strawberries then add to rhubarb and cook for another 5 minutes. Store in clean jars and process in hot water bath for 10 minutes. Use recycled jars with tops that "pop" (those that when you first open them, you know they were sealed). If in doubt, use new lids. Usually, I don't measure anything when I make jam; generally, I just add the fruit and sugar and occasionally some citrus zest or peel or agar agar to thicken it. It's so easy, and you can control how much/little sugar you want to use.

No Pectin Blueberry Jam

I discovered how to make blueberry jam without pectin because I didn't have any on hand and really wanted to make it. Turned out great! Makes a really thick jam, so if you want it thinner, consider cooking it for 30 minutes instead.

Ingredients:

- blueberries
- sugar
- lemon juice

Instructions:

Use the same amount of crushed blueberries as sugar. I used 4 cups of crushed berries and 4 cups of sugar and ended up with 4 jars of jam. Use about 1 tablespoon of lemon juice. Add everything in a heavy saucepan, bring to a boil, and stir. Once it comes to a roaring boil, turn the heat down to low, stirring every

10 minutes or so, making sure the berries are still slowly boiling. Boil for about 45 minutes or until the thermometer reaches 220°F. Pour into hot sterilized glass jars, tighten the lid, and turn upside down for 15 minutes. This is just easier than using the water bath method and works! If some lids don't "pop," store in the refrigerator for 4 weeks.

Mystery Berry Jam

This is a great jam for all the leftover berries you have. I had a handful of raspberries leftover from my garden late August, a few cups of blueberries someone gave me from the wild, and a handful of blackberries. You can use any combination! The key is to crush all the berries you have, then measure. Use the same amount of sugar as what you have in crushed berries. Add 1 tablespoon lemon juice. Put everything in a heavy saucepan, bring to a roaring boil, turn down heat, and let boil for 30 minutes, stirring every 6 to 10 minutes or so to prevent burning. If you want a really thick jam, boil for 45 minutes, especially if you have more blueberries than other berries! MMMMMMMMMMMM.

Spring/Summer Sweet Treats

Rhubarb Crunch

Seeing rhubarb in the garden is definitely the first sign of spring for me!! Here is one of my favorite rhubarb things to make.

Ingredients:

- 1 cup flour (I use spelt)
- ¾ cups rolled oats
- ½ cup brown sugar
- ½ teaspoon salt

- 1 teaspoon cinnamon
- ½ cup melted margarine

Instructions:
Combine all this stuff in a medium bowl and blend with a fork until crumbly.

Put 4 cups rhubarb in an 8 x 8" pan.

In a saucepan combine:

- ¾ cup sugar
- 2 tablespoons cornstarch
- 1 cup hot water

Heat until thick, then add 1 teaspoon vanilla and stir.

Pour syrup over rhubarb, sprinkle crumb mix on top, and bake at 325°F for 50 mins.

Date Bars

Lots of people seem really into fancy and expensive brand-name date bars. When I looked at the ingredients, I thought that I could reproduce something similar myself. After some failed attempts, here is the prize winner:

Ingredients and Instructions:
Start with 2 cups dates (if you keep yours in the fridge like I do, soak them for a minute in warm water). Blend in a food processor, then transfer to a bowl and add:

- ¼ cup chopped walnuts
- ¼ cup chopped almonds
- ¼ cup unsweetened coconut
- (some carob or cocoa powder if you wish)

Form into 6 bars and refrigerate, then wrap individually.

Makes 6 1-ounce bars. This cost me around 50¢ a bar, if not cheaper. Great to take on hikes or if you're hitching around the country and need to pack light, energy-packed snacks!

Walter's Dutch Pancakes

My sweetie makes the easiest, cheapest, and best pancakes in the world! They are actually thin like French crepes, and you fill them, roll them up with goodies, and eat them.

When my sweetie was growing up in Holland as a child, most kids had these at birthday parties (which I find better than the pizza and cake people serve in North America—eek!). The parents would make them as it was inexpensive, and the kids would have lots of fun filling them with stuff!

Ingredients:

- flour
- non-dairy milk/water or both
- vanilla extract
- various fillings (sugar, maple syrup, fruit, cheese, etc.)

Instructions:

Add a few cups of flour (whole unbleached, spelt), then using a whisk, start adding water/milk until you get a thin but not-too-runny batter (not as thick as you would have it for North American pancakes). Once you have the right consistency, add a little vanilla (or even cinnamon if you wish!) and mix. Heat a non-stick large skillet, add a little margarine, then using a soup ladle, pour mix into pan and move the pan around until the bottom is entirely coated with the batter. Should be quite thin. Wait a few minutes, then turn the pancake over and cook for another minute or so. Keep doing this until all the batter is gone. I find that the first one is always a bit sketchy. Fill the middle with toppings such as icing sugar (poeder suiker, which is a Dutch favorite), brown sugar, chocolate chips, fresh fruit, maple syrup, or even vegan cheese! YUM!

Summer Baked Goods

Oatmeal Chocolate Chip Muffins

Ingredients:

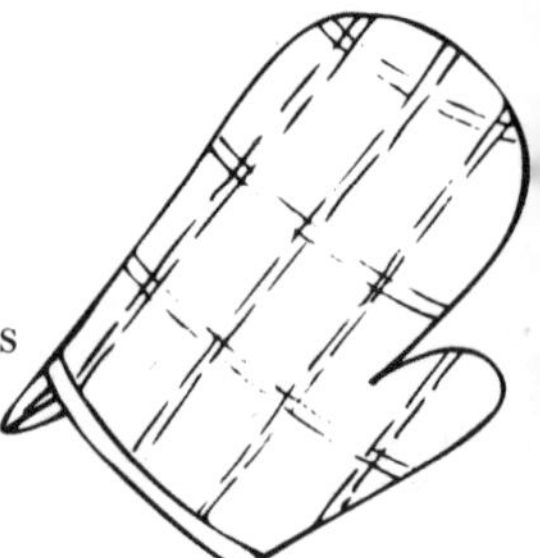

- ½ cup canola oil
- 1 cup lightly packed brown sugar
- 1 vegan egg replacement
- 1 cup soymilk mixed with 2 teaspoons vinegar
- 2 cups flour
- 1 teaspoon baking soda
- 1 teaspoons baking powder
- ½ teaspoon salt
- 1 teaspoon vanilla
- 1 cup oats
- ¾ cup chocolate chips

Instructions:

Preheat the oven to 400°F. Line a muffin tray with muffin cups and spray them with cooking spray. Combine the canola oil, brown sugar, egg, vanilla, and buttermilk. Mix well. Combine the flour, baking soda, baking powder, salt, chocolate chips, and oats. Mix together until just blended. Spoon into the muffin cups. Bake about 25 minutes.

Applesauce Rum-Raisin Cake

Ingredients:

- 2 cups flour (I use light spelt)
- 1 teaspoon baking soda
- 1 teaspoon cinnamon
- ½ teaspoon cloves
- ½ teaspoon nutmeg or allspice
- ½ cup margarine
- 1 cup sugar
- 1 teaspoon vanilla
- ½ ripe banana (or your fave egg replacer = 1 egg)
- 1 ¼ cups applesauce (unsweetened)
- 1 cup raisins
- ⅓ cup rum (I use vanilla rum)

Instructions:

Soak raisins in rum for at least an hour. Though, I have gotten away with only soaking them for 10 minutes, and it worked out fine.

In a small bowl, mix flour, soda, and spices. In a large bowl, mix margarine, sugar, vanilla, and banana until smooth. Beat in the flour to the margarine mixture alternately with the applesauce. Add raisins, including any leftover rum. Bake at 325°F until a toothpick inserted comes out clean. About 30 to 40 minutes.

Strawberry Rhubarb Crisp

First time I made this, I brought it to a potluck and it got devoured! Easy to make and so super delicious!

Ingredients:

- 3 cups diced rhubarb
- 3 cups sliced strawberries
- 1 cup sugar
- 3 tablespoons flour
- ½ teaspoon cinnamon (optional)
- 1 ½ cups flour
- 1 cup oats
- ½ cup margarine
- 1 cup packed brown sugar

Instructions:

Preheat oven to 350°F.

In a large bowl, mix fruit, sugar, flour, and cinnamon (if using). Spread evenly in a 9 x 13–inch baking pan. In another bowl, mix all other ingredients. Crumble on top of fruit and bake for 40 to 45 minutes.

Raspberry Bars

These are so easy to make and you can replace the raspberry jam with whatever fruit jam you have on hand!

Ingredients:

- ½ cup brown sugar
- 1 cup flour
- 1 cup rolled oats
- ¼ teaspoon baking soda
- ⅛ teaspoon sea salt

- ½ cup margarine
- ¾ cup jam (raspberry or other kind)

Instructions:
Mix the first 5 ingredients, then add margarine and mix with a fork until the mixture becomes crumbly.

In a foil-lined greased 8 x 8–inch pan, spread 2 cups of the mixture and press down to pack it. Then, spread jam on top. Put the rest of the mixture on top and spread lightly, don't press. Bake at 350°F for 35 to 40 minutes. Cool, then cut! Serve to hungry friends.

Granola Bars

One of my many concoctions that turned out so yummy!

Ingredients:

- 2 cups oatmeal
- ⅓ cup sunflower seeds
- ⅓ cup sesame seeds
- handful of raisins
- handful of chocolate chips
- handful of shredded coconut
- 2 to 3 tablespoons peanut butter
- maple, pomegranate, and brown rice syrup

Instructions:
Preheat the oven to 350°F.

Blend all dry ingredients in a bowl. Add peanut butter and a few drizzles of each syrup and blend well. Add more syrup if needed, as you want the batter to be moist and stick together.

In an 8 x 8 greased baking pan, pat down mix and bake for about 15 minutes or until lightly browned on top.

Tip: You can buy pomegranate syrup at middle eastern grocery stores. If you don't have it, use any other type of fruit or malt syrup or grenadine.

Fall
and
Winter

INTRODUCTION

Everyone knows that winter can be tough, long, and cold. Keeping this in mind, I dug into some of my archives and found a lot of interesting info and ideas to make this fall and winter more bearable and affordable. In this special booklet, you will find recipes, tips, and more! Since this is the fall and winter section, most of the recipes use seasonal fruits and veggies, as it's always best to cook with the seasons! Hope you enjoy it!

FRUGAL ACTIVITIES AND TIPS

Egg Replacer Ideas

Eggs are generally used as a binder in cooking/baking and are easily and cheaply replaced in recipes. Here are a few to try:

Soy Flour or Cornstarch Mix

Mix 1 tablespoon soy flour or cornstarch with 2 tablespoons water. Mix well. This equals 1 egg.

Flaxseed Mix

Mix 1 tablespoon ground flaxseed with 3 tablespoons warm water. Let sit for 10 minutes, then add to recipe. This equals 1 egg.

Banana Mash

Mash ½ a large banana. This equals 1 egg.

Preserving Fall Leaves

You will need:

- dried leaves
- floor wax
- bowl
- newspaper
- wax paper
- old catalog or phonebook
- old or inexpensive paint brushes

Instructions:

Gather some pretty fall leaves once they have fallen. Lay newspapers down on a work surface. Pour some wax into the bowl. Carefully brush wax onto the leaves. This will make them shiny. To dry, place them between 2 pieces of wax paper and place between a catalog or phonebook pages. Use to make cards or decorate the windows and doors!

Bartering for Survival

Most of us are broke around now and after the holidays (or always for that matter?). The problem is, we all need a haircut every now and again, some food to feed our hungry bellies, heat to keep us warm, and some interesting cheap stuff to do to pass the time on those long dark cold days! So, what do we do? Barter!

I've recently started to barter with people for things I need or would like to have—even small things.

I have the pleasure of knowing some fantastic people who love to barter with me. Myself, I make all kinds of soap and bath stuff and have just started studying Reiki and aromatherapy, so I can offer any of those things to people who would like to barter with me. I recently mentioned the bartering idea to a colleague of mine who replied, "Well, I have nothing to offer, I have no talents or hobbies that I could offer." Upon talking to her a little longer, I found out some things about her that she didn't think could be bartered. Apparently, she keeps a super clean apartment and compared herself to Monica from *Friends*.

I mentioned someone could give a free massage if she cleaned their apartment? Her eyes widened with sudden interest, and she seriously started thinking about the possibilities of this old but useful concept.

If you live in Canada, you've probably seen that commercial: "No one is good at everything, but everyone is good at something." Maybe you don't mind shoveling snow, babysitting, house sitting, gardening, or even doing laundry! Let's face it, all of us like doing something someone else doesn't right? So you don't need to be a carpenter, hairstylist, or master chef to barter!

Okay, you're in a bind: You desperately need a haircut, however, all your friends are capable of is giving you bowl cuts or shave your head. Problem is, you still have nightmares about those bow cuts your mom used to give you when you were a kid, and you used to shave your head years ago but you've decided to keep some hair this year. What to do? Post a sign somewhere (e.g., school, work) that states that you are willing to do (e.g., clean, babysit) if someone would cut your hair (make sure they have scissor training).

Also, ask around, because friends of friends might know someone. I know what you're thinking: seems like a lot of hassle for a $10 haircut! But hey, that was just an example. And second of all, wouldn't you want to save that $10?

Make Your Domain Smell as Sweet as Pie

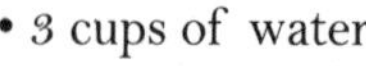

Don't want to bake a pie but want your place to smell like you are??

In a small saucepan, turn heat on low.

Add the following:

- 3 cups of water
- 5 to 6 cloves
- 1 stick of cinnamon, broken into pieces
- 1 small apple chopped, not peeled or cored (or saved apple cores—recycled!)
- some orange or lemon peels, if you have them around

After 15 to 20 minutes, you'll start to smell the yummy scent traveling through your apartment/house. Make sure you don't forget about it though! A safer thing to do would be to use your crockpot for this. (Saves energy too!)

You can also add more water after most of it has evaporated.

Cheap-o Gift Wrapping Ideas

Most of these wrapping ideas are recycled ones. You may think some of them are a bit off the wall, but people certainly won't accuse you of being unoriginal!

Cut chip bags into strips to use as ribbon! Chip bags are usually metallic on the inside so it makes funky ribbon.

Use brown paper bags and decorate with stickers and ink stamps. I know it sounds kitsch, but people love it because it is!

Use the comic section of the newspaper or pages of glossy magazines to wrap gifts. You could even use the travel or another section of a newspaper that might be appropriate for the receiver.

Sew your own gift pouches! I'm pretty bad at sewing, but I can make these. Cut one large piece of material double the size you want your bag. Fold in half and iron it to keep it in place. Fold over about 1 inch of the side you want your string to go in. Sew that. Then, sew the two sides inside out, and put your cord through the top! Voila!

Decorate a recycled paper bag with a red string and nature's gifts: pinecones, pine needles, autumn leaves, dried flowers, etc. You could also glue on buttons!

Visit your local thrift store and purchase baskets, tins, and loose material to use as wrapping.

Purchase Tupperware-style containers at the dollar or thrift store and fill with presents! The receiver always appreciates this because the container is reusable. No waste!

If you are giving high-up gifts, wrap the goodies in a towel and tie with ribbon. Towels can be purchased at the dollar or thrift store.

Cut up old jeans, dresses, or shirts that you were just about to throw away, and wrap your presents in this! Cut strips of fabric to use as ribbon.

Decorate with a collage of scrap material (purchased at thrift stores, or given to you by a friend/family who sews).

Crocheted Cloths/Towels: My mom makes me a bunch of these so I can wrap my handmade soaps in them. You may also make larger towels and wrap a bunch of things in there; toiletries and bath goods would be good. Or, if you make/buy a kitchen towel, you can use that to wrap kitchen-related gifts.

Use crocheted cloths/towels. My mom makes me a bunch of these so I can wrap my handmade soaps in them.

Try a pillowcase! I've always found myself with a lot of extra pillowcases because I find a lot in the thrift store. These can be used for bigger gifts or if you want to fill a bag full of goodies. What is nice is that it can be used again when all the gifts are out of it.

Used cookie tins make great packaging for your homemade goods or even just any type of present. Tins come in so many shapes and sizes as well and are easily found in thrift stores. Also, check with family members—I am sure Grandma has tons.

Make your own gift tags with recycled cards! Do you receive a lot of holiday cards? It's time to put them to use! Just cut the cover of the card into small squares and use them as gift tags. Usually, people don't write messages right behind the front of the card. You can also do this with any type of card you have received (birthday, Halloween, etc.).

Frugal Holiday Gifts

No matter what you celebrate (or don't celebrate for that matter), sometimes you want to give people gifts around the holidays. People spend a crapload of money on useless junk! Don't support consumerism: make your own stuff.

(One year I was really lazy and didn't end up making the usual bath stuff and candles I normally make. I also bake for people, but that didn't happen either. I ended up going to dollar stores and making bags with a collection of stuff like candles, candy, and incense. Don't be like me—start early and make gifts because it's worth it. Homemade is best, trust me!)

The beauty of homemade gifts is that you create them yourself with your positive energy and love! They are always unique and special. Lots of people think that making your own gifts makes you look cheap! But if someone thinks that about your fab homemade gift, then they don't deserve to be friends with you, right? In my experience, family and friends actually look forward to what I am making them each year! Making your own gifts is also a great way to save cash—for those who don't want to spend money, or don't have it.

This section is for you. From picky relatives to friends who "have it all," this section will have something for everyone.

Eye Makeup Remover

Ingredients:

- 1 tablespoon castor oil
- 1 tablespoon light olive oil
- 2 teaspoons canola oil

Instructions:

Blend the above ingredients together. Apply with tissue or a cotton ball to remove makeup around the eyes.

Bath Salts (General)

- 1 cup fine sea salt
- ½ cup epsom salts
- ¼ cup baking soda
- 2 teaspoons dried herbs, optional
- 10 to 15 drops of essential oil

Mix all ingredients and spread on wax paper. Let dry for a few hours. Store in plastic bags or glass jars.

Rose Bath Salts

Ingredients:

- 1 cup coarse sea salt
- ½ cup baking soda
- small handful of crushed rose petals (maybe ½ cup?)
- 20 drops of rose essential oil (optional)

Instructions:

Mix the sea salt, baking soda, and petals. Add rose essential oil (optional). Store in a clear glass container.

For use, add ¼ cup bath salt and ¼ cup rose water to bathwater.

Another Option: green tea bath—same as above but add loose green tea.

Bath Beads

Ingredients:

- 2 tablespoons baking soda
- 1 teaspoon vegetable shortening
- 10 drops fragrance or essential oil

Instructions:

Mix all ingredients and knead into balls. Let air dry for 24 hours.

Digestive Aromatherapy Blend

Add 4 ounces of sea salts to a bowl and mix with:

- 1 drop ginger essential oil
- 2 drops peppermint essential oil
- 6 drops orange essential oil

Place a candle in the middle and light after a meal. This blend helps with digestion. Use therapeutic-grade oils.

Chakra Balancing Oil

For friends who meditate, do yoga, or whose chakras need a little balancing!

Ingredients:

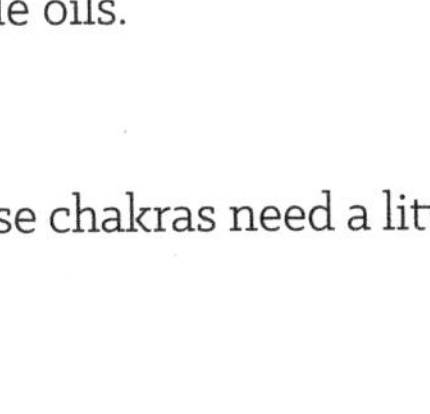

- ¼ cup almond oil
- 10 drops patchouli
- 5 drops sandalwood
- 3 drops tangerine

Instructions:

Add all ingredients and mix well. Store in a dark glass bottle. Dab on wrists, neck, or anywhere on your body.

Stones for Each Chakra

Root: red jasper

Sacral: carnelian

Solar Plexus: citrine

Heart: aventurine

Throat: moonstone

Third Eye: amethyst

Crown: rock crystal

Tip: Place all stones in a small pouch. Now you have a chakra balancing bag!

Scrapbooks

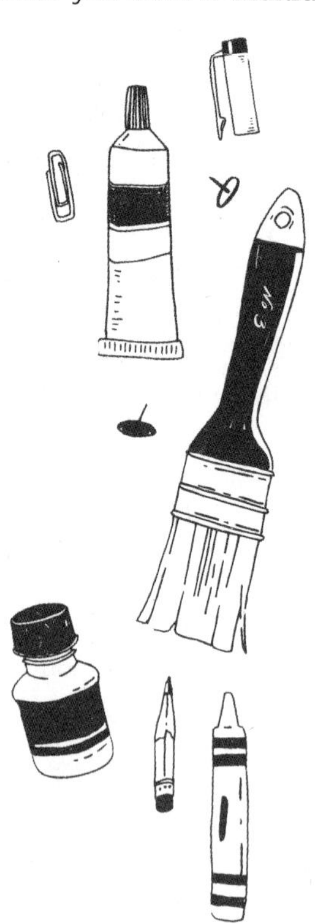

A lot of housewives are into this stuff, but you don't need to make them all frilly and colorful. You can make super cool scrapbooks for people out of paper bags.

Tips for Scrapbooks:

- Use scrap materials to decorate.
- For lettering, use cutouts from magazines, alphabet stickers, or print stuff out on the computer.
- Start early; collect photos, sayings, quotes, or whatever inspires you.
- Work on it bit by bit. The more you make, the better you get!
- Having a theme like "Friends" or "Our Road Trip" can make it easier and more inspiring.

Thrift Store Clothes

I found a lovely t-shirt for a friend while thrift store shopping in the fall. It was perfect, and I kept it until December for the holidays. If you see something a friend or family member would love, grab it—even if it's months in advance. If you're unsure about sizes, gift them a thrift store gift certificate.

Bubble Bags

Ingredients:

- 2 parts oatmeal
- 2 parts dried herbs (lavender, chamomile, mint, etc.)
- 1 part grated soap

Instructions:

Place ingredients in a cloth bag and use as a washcloth.

Hemp (Macrame) Bracelets

You will need . . .

- assorted beads with holes large enough to fit over 2 strings
- leather crimps and clasps
- string or cord

Prepare the Strings:

Cut 2 strings 2 inches longer than the length of the finished project (these are the 2 center strings).

Cut 2 strings that are 3 ½ times longer than the first 2 strings (these are the 2 outside strings).

Steps to Knotting:

Step 1: Make a "4" shape over the 2 center strings with the leftside string.

Step 2: Move the rightside string over the tail of the "4," under the 2 center strings, and then through the triangle of the "4."

Step 3: Tighten the knot by pulling the 2 side strings while holding the center strings.

Adding Beads:

String the beads on the 2 center strings and macrame around the beads.

Continue repeating the knot until the project is completed.

Optional Styles:

Twisting rope: Repeat the knot in the same direction with every knot.

Flat rope: Alternate starting on the right, then the left side, with each knot.

To Attach the Clasp:

Pull the last knot tight.

Cut the strings to ¾ cm tails.

Put all 4 tails into the leather crimp with the loop pointing outwards.

Fold over the sides of the leather crimps with pliers and attach the clasps.

CD Compilations

Create a CD compilation as a gift for special friends or family. Compile music that is special to you and the receiver. Add a story or memory to each song (e.g., "Remember when we heard this over and over again when we took our trip to Australia together?").

Aftershave Gel

This recipe is perfect for all skin types. Vodka and witch hazel help tone the skin without irritation.

Ingredients:

- ½ cup aloe vera gel
- 2 tablespoons vodka
- 1 tablespoon orange flower water
- 2 teaspoons witch hazel
- 10 drops sandalwood essential oil (or lavender)

Instructions:

Combine all ingredients in a bottle and shake well until blended.

Eau de Linge (Laundry Spray)

A luxurious gift!

Ingredients:

- 1 liter dark glass or plastic bottle
- 1 liter distilled water
- 100 drops lavender essential oil
- 5 drops peppermint essential oil
- ¼ cup pure vodka

Instructions:

Mix vodka and essential oils in the bottle and shake well.

Add distilled water and shake again.

To use, add ¼ cup to the rinse cycle. This makes your clothes smell terrific!

As a gift idea, include a muslin bag filled with dried lavender flowers. Add the bag to the dryer when drying clothes.

Personal Coupons

If you're really broke and can't purchase anything for the holidays, consider giving personal coupons. For example, you could give coupons such as:

- baby/pet sitting (good for XX hours/days)
- mowing the lawn (in summer, of course!)
- cooking a meal
- foot massage
- walking the dog
- house sitting

Put an expiry date on the coupon as well! You can handwrite them or print them out on the computer.

Clove-Studded Oranges

These make the room smell fabulous, and as an added bonus, they repel moths! Make some for yourself or give them away for the holidays.

Purchase cloves at a bulk store (East Indian or Middle Eastern stores are cheaper to buy there). Also, purchase discounted oranges from your grocery or health food store. If they are not out on display, ask the produce manager for some.

Materials:

- oranges
- cloves
- ribbon or drawstring bag

Instructions:

Use a small nail to poke holes in the orange and push the cloves in.

Pack them tightly and use a thimble if necessary.

Allow to dry for 2 weeks, then tie with a ribbon to hang or put in a drawstring bag to use in drawers.

Kitchen Sink Simmering Pot-Pourri

A cheap-o gift using stuff you'd otherwise chuck in your compost!

Ingredients:

- dried apple peels
- whole cloves
- dried orange and lemon peels
- cinnamon sticks, broken into pieces
- dried whole ginger (just use the old stuff you forgot about in your fridge)
- pinecones from your yard (optional, but looks cool)

Instructions:

Make sure all fruits are dried. To do that, place everything on a cookie sheet and dehydrate in an oven at 200°F for several hours.

Toss all your goodies in a bowl and package in clear cellophane, or plastic bags, or a clear jar.

To use:

Put some of the mix in a few cups of water and simmer on the lowest heat.

Citrus Anti-Depression Bath

Citrus oils are known to uplift your mood. This is a perfect bath for a dark, cold night when you've had enough of winter! These make amazing, unique gifts.

Ingredients:

- 1 orange
- 1 grapefruit
- 1 lime

- 1 lemon
- 1 tangerine
- Almond, sunflower, or grapeseed oil

Instructions:

Try to find citrus fruits that are discounted for this!

Feel free to use a few of the same fruits if that's all you have.

Slice each fruit into thin slices and place on several cookie sheets.

Dry in a warm (200°F) oven for many hours until dry, or leave slices in the oven (turned off) for several weeks.(This would be more frugal, but also more time-consuming.)

Once the slices are completely dry, package about 10 to 15 slices of mixed fruits in cellophane bags and add a small glass bottle with 1 tablespoon of oil.

Tie with ribbon and give as gifts!

To use:

Place all fruit slices in the bath along with oil and soak! If you want the citrus bath right away, use the fresh fruit slices. This bath luxury definitely looks awesome and is incredibly uplifting.

Brownies in a Bag

Fun gift for friends who don't like to bake.

Ingredients:

- ¾ cup cocoa
- 1 ½ cups flour
- ½ teaspoon baking soda
- ½ teaspoon salt
- 2 cups sugar
- 2 tablespoons cornstarch

Instructions:

Mix cocoa and soda together well. Add other dry ingredients.

Store in a plastic baggie or recycled coffee bean paper bags.

Decorate with funky stickers and ribbons. Follow directions on the tag.

Tag Instructions:

Add ¾ cup + 2 tablespoons boiling water to dry ingredients.

Stir in ⅔ cup oil and 1 teaspoon vanilla.

Pour in lightly greased 9 x 13–inch pan and bake at 350°F for 35 to 40 minutes.

Dancing Damiana Dream Tea

A perfect "before bed" tea. This makes a great gift too. Package in a clear jar and attach a metal tea ball with it!

Ingredients:

- ¼ cup damiana leaves
- ¼ cup chamomile flowers
- ¼ cup lemongrass leaves
- ¼ cup spearmint leaves
- 1 tablespoon jasmine flowers
- 1 tablespoon dried orange peels

Instructions:

Mix all ingredients and store in a clean jar. To make: Add 1 teaspoon to tea ball. Add tea ball to mug, pour 1 cup boiling water over it, and steep for 5 to 10 minutes.

Microwave Butter Toffee

Ingredients:

- 1 ⅓ cup sugar
- 1 cup softened butter
- 2 tablespoons water
- 1 tablespoon dark corn syrup
- 1 teaspoon vanilla
- ¾ cup semisweet chocolate chips
- ⅔ cup chopped walnuts

Instructions:

In a large microwave-safe bowl, mix sugar, butter, water, and corn syrup.

Microwave on high for 4 minutes, stirring every 2 minutes.

Heat 6 to 8 minutes longer until thickened and gold in color.

Add vanilla and stir well.

Pour mixture into a 9 x 13–inch dish.

Spread chocolate chips over hot toffee and sprinkle with nuts.

Cool completely. Break into pieces.

Apple Oatmeal Bars

Friends coming over last minute?? These bars are so easy, quick, and cheap to make! Everyone will think you spent hours making these because they taste so delicious.

Ingredients:

- 1 cup oatmeal
- ½ teaspoon salt
- ½ cup margarine
- 1 cup flour
- 1 teaspoon cinnamon

- 2 ½ cups chopped apples
- ½ cup sugar

Instructions:

Combine the first 5 ingredients and mix well.

Put half of the mixture into an 8 x 8 pan.

Sprinkle apples and sugar on top. Pat the other half of the mixture on top of apples, and press down a little.

Bake at 350°F for 30 to 35 minutes.

Gift Basket Ideas

Purchase your baskets at thrift stores! Reuse and recycle. Read the Cheap-o Gift Wrapping Ideas section on how to wrap your basket goodies.

Newbie Vegan Pack

This is great for friends who are just newly vegan or are in the process of becoming vegan. Show your support!

- 1 copy of this book or a local vegan zine
- A few bags of seeds, nuts, and beans. Feel free to attach recipes to the bags!
- 1 package of nutritional yeast (A must-have for vegans!)
- 1 bag of TVP granules (attach recipes if needed)

Stressed-Out Mama Basket

Do you have friends who are always on the go? Can't relax? This is for them!

- 1 eye pillow
- 1 bag of bath salts
- 1 bottle of chakra balancing oil

- 1 CD (your own compilation with relaxation music—meditation, yoga)
- 1 votive candle

You can also include your own little sheet on how to relax using the items in the basket. Suggestions:

Soak in the bath with a votive candle listening to relaxing music.

Massage a little chakra balancing oil before heading out for a busy day.

When you get home, unwind with a warmed-up eye pillow.

Valentine's Day Gifts and Ideas

I rarely give in to commercial holidays, especially Valentine's Day! Damn consumerism!

The past few years, I decided to have fun with it instead—kitsch it up! The following homemade gifts are some ideas from those festive adventures.

Simple Gestures Done in an Elaborate Way

One year, my partner gave me the following gift: he handed me a pile of papers. The first page said, "It's your birthday, and I am going to take care of you." Each subsequent page listed the next part of the experience, such as serving me tea, giving me a foot bath, and cooking me dinner. It was memorable and cost nothing but time and thought!

Overnight Sex Kit

This idea was inspired by a friend. You can make it fun or serious.

Contents:

- 1 condom (glow in the dark, flavored)
- 1 sample lube (the warming stuff is cool)
- 1 small votive candle
- 1 sample cologne or perfume
- 1 mini bottle of booze
- 1 wipe (moist wipe for cleanup; your local sex shop will have these)
- optional additions: gum and a disposable toothbrush

Cook Dinner

Cooking for someone is a sexy and personal gift. Use recipes from this book. Decorate the table with a few inexpensive white and red or pink candles and a single flower in a vase. Food is the sexiest gift ever!

Valentine's Goody Bags

These are great gifts for friends. Fill small bags with:

- candles
- homemade baked goods
- perfume samples (free ones!)
- heart candies

You can stuff a bag full of fun items for under $5 by looking around for freebies.

Write a Story/Poem

Are you a decent writer or poet? Write about when you first met your partner or create goofy poetry like this:

Roses Are Red
Violets Are Blue
You're hot in bed
And I love you.

Remember, have fun with it!

Cinnamon Pinecones

These are great to display in a bowl or throw in your fireplace for a lovely aroma! I've seen these at stores for $10! Geez! Make your own and give them as gifts.

Instructions:

Boil 5 cinnamon sticks in a medium-sized pot of water for 5 to 10 minutes.

Add pinecones and let sit as the water cools.

Lay pinecones on a rack to dry.

Body Sundae in a Box

This is a fun gift if you have a playful lover! In a small box from the dollar store, put in the following:

- cinnamon hearts
- chocolate sprinkles
- canned whipped cream
- chocolate sauce

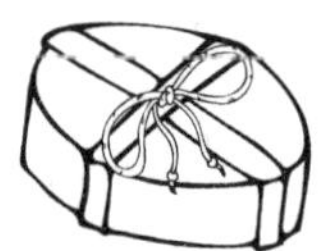

Label the box something fun like "A Body Sundae for You." To use, light a candle, and cover your body with whipped cream, candy, and sauce. Mmmm!

Staying Away From Tradition and Tacky Romance

Avoid doing/buying the following:

- Don't Buy Roses: Opt for a nice plant instead—it'll last longer.
- Don't Buy Lingerie: Unless it's just for fun, and you get cheap novelty ones.
- Don't Go to Fancy Restaurants: Stay home and cook a personal meal instead.
- Don't Buy Stuffed Animals or Heart-Shaped Candy Boxes: Bake cookies or give something meaningful instead.
- Don't Buy Expensive Spa Gift Certificates: Choose aesthetic schools instead—cheaper and just as good.
- Don't Purchase Perfume or Jewelry: Make homemade bath salts or get edible candy necklaces.

Advice: Showing affection doesn't come from your wallet!

Valentine's Surprises: Under 10 Minutes and $10

If you're not much of a crafter, writer, cook, or baker, you can do simple, easy gestures that take little time and money but will be much appreciated (some are tacky but can be fun):

- Surprise your lover at work/school with a coffee and a cookie/muffin.
- Spread fake rose petals ($3 to $4) on the bed and light some candles.
- Draw a bath for your special person(s) with new bubblebath you bought for them, bring them a cup of tea, and sponge them clean.
- Text message their cell phone or send a sweet email every hour for a few hours.

- Get a mug from the Salvation Army with hearts on it (I've seen these for 20¢), fill with coffee beans or chocolate, and gift it.
- Buy a rose plant or small rose for about $4.

Keeping Warm On-the-Cheap

We keep our thermostat at seventeen degrees Celsius most of the time, and fifteen at night. It's a little chilly in here, so we bought two small portable heaters. We'll turn one on in the room we're sitting in, and/or cover up with blankets or sweaters. This saves A LOT of money. You don't ever have to heat the entire house. We also turn off the radiators in the rooms we're rarely in.

When I'm really cold and don't want to turn the heat up, I take a super hot bath. It keeps me warm until I have to go to bed. If you don't want to waste water, fill a small basin with hot water and soak your feet; that will help a lot.

I tend to enjoy drinking hot beverages when I am cold. Warm up with a hot cup of ginger tea. Works wonders, especially if you use fresh ginger. Just boil a pot of water, throw in some grated ginger, and voila. Sweeten with agave nectar or honey, if you use it.

Cover up older windows with that plastic stuff you can buy at the hardware store. It works! Ask them about it; it doesn't cost too much and you'll save on your heating bill.

Wear a hat. By wearing a hat indoors, you'll stay warm. Buy a funky hat at the thrift store! In my old apartment (which was in an old house, poorly insulated), I also wore mittens sometimes—kind of inconvenient, but it works if you're frozen and can't afford the heating bill.

I keep blankets in almost every room. They're handy. Do it.

An electric blanket might be a good idea if you don't want to use portable heaters, which can also make your electric bill slightly higher than normal. They can be expensive, but you'll get your money back in a year for sure. I've seen them at thrift stores but was a bit wary of buying one used. I buy a lot of used stuff, but the ones I saw were old and quite frankly, I don't want to run the risk of setting myself on fire. Buy them when the sales are best.

Save Money and Get Out of Debt

Okay, so you're in debt and you're living paycheck to paycheck. Seems like so many of us are! It's hard to save when you constantly have debts hanging over you. A lot of us are totally broke a day or two before we get paid. So what now??

Transfer to a lower rate credit card or get a prepaid one! Credit card balances are what's killing a lot of us.

Put yourself on a budget. Give yourself $50 a week for stuff. Keep cash and never use your debit card. I do this, and my account is just used for payments. This REALLY works!

Sell junk you don't need or use anymore. I made about $350 one week after spring cleaning and posting stuff on Craigslist.

Buy secondhand. I read about a group in San Francisco that decided collectively not to purchase anything new for one year (except for toiletries and food). It started as an environmental project, but many of them paid off debts during this experiment. Use thrift stores, dumpster diving, and Freecycle to find items you need without spending much (or any!) money.

Save water. Fill a 1-liter plastic bottle with water and install it in your toilet tank. This will reduce the amount of water being used per flush.

Use recycled packaging. Use shredded paper (we have a shredder next to our computer) instead of foam peanuts or bubble wrap to pack a box or envelope!

Drink at home! I like going out but can't afford the bar prices. So I have drinks at home with a few friends, then share a cab over (or walk if it's nice out!). We get there right before the drinks go up in price, buy one, and that's it. The other week I got a ride there and back for free and spent only $13 (cover and one drink). I also tend to drink enough before I go out so that I don't want to drink more . . . hehe.

Picture these savings: After spending $3.99 plus tax for frame hangers, I figured there's got to be another way! There is! In a pinch, you can use the pop-top from an aluminum soda can. Picture frames that are under about two pounds will hold up nicely. Remove the pop-top by turning it slightly and applying steady pressure until the top pops off. Small wood screws or tiny nails with larger heads will fit nicely. Just attach the pop-top to the top middle of the frame and hang the picture as usual.

Get energy-saving bulbs. I found these energy-saving bulbs at the dollar store! You can also get them in combo packs of 6 for about $10. Change all your regular bulbs; this will save you quite a bit a year!

Cut your food bills in half. Don't buy lunch at work; brown-bag it! Buy dry, not canned, beans and purchase in bulk when possible. Shop for seasonal specials for freshness and savings. Avoid eating out more than once a week, if at all, and go to places offering discounts like 2-for-1 coupons or cheap meals.

Make a sock dispenser. Socks have a life after death. Take old socks and put a hole at the toe end. Sew a ring of elastic into that hole with needle and thread. Next, get a small screw and large washer and screw the sock into a kitchen sink door or a similar location. Place rolled-up plastic bags into the sock on one end and use it as a dispenser for trash bags. Or, instead of using a ton of paper towels, use small clean rags the size of washcloths. Bundle them each into a knot and put them into the sock dispenser. When you need a paper towel, reach for a rag instead. Toss the dirty rags into a plastic bag and send them with the laundry. Dispose of any rag with chemicals or painting products into a closed metal container. They can spontaneously ignite, as my friend found out one day—one garage later! Save a bundle on paper towels and trash bags.

RECIPES

Warm up and celebrate the cooler months with your loved ones with these delightful and practical vegan recipes rooted in the season!

Drinks to Warm Your Bod

Ginger Lemon Tea

Ingredients:

- 4 cups water
- 1 tablespoon minced ginger
- Half of an organic lemon, sliced

Instructions:

In a small saucepan, combine water, ginger, and lemon. Simmer on low for about 20 minutes. Strain. Sweeten with your favorite sweetener.

Super Chocolaty Hot Cocoa Mix

Ingredients:

- ¼ cup dried soy milk powder
- ¼ cup non-dairy powdered creamer
- ½ cup powdered sugar
- ¼ cup cocoa powder (or carob)

Instructions:

Mix all ingredients in a blender to ensure that they are fully blended. Store in a glass jar in a cool place.

To make, add 3 tablespoons of mix to 1 cup hot water. TIP! If you wish to make a Mochaccino Mix, add ¼ cup or so of instant coffee! Mmmmmnnn!

Achy Tummy Tea

Have you eaten too many yummy vegan delicacies this holiday season? Make this tea and soothe your achy tummy!

Ingredients:

- ½ cup dried peppermint leaves
- ½ tablespoon dried rosemary
- ½ tablespoon dried sage

Instructions:

Crush ingredients and mix well. Store in a tightly closed container. Steep 1 heaping teaspoon in 1 cup of boiling water for 2 minutes. Sweeten to taste.

Honey Lemon Soother

I drink this when my throat gets sore. This happens especially when the seasons change. Drink 2 to 3 times a day until you feel better.

Ingredients:

- 1 ½ cups hot water
- 1 slice of lemon
- 1 teaspoon honey

Instructions:

Blend all ingredients in a large mug and let steep for 3 to 5 minutes.

Hot Spiced Wine

Ingredients:

- 1 bottle full-bodied red wine
- 3 tablespoons honey
- 2 cinnamon sticks
- 2 tablespoons cardamom seeds
- 1 tablespoon black peppercorns
- 1 sliced orange
- 1 sliced lemon
- ½ cup sugar

Instructions:

Combine all ingredients in a saucepan. Simmer for 15 minutes. Serve warm.

Holiday Breakfast

Banana Pumpkin Shake

Ingredients:

- 1 cup soy or rice milk
- 2 tablespoons pumpkin mush
- 1 banana
- dash of cinnamon

Instructions:

Blend in blender until smooth and foamy. Serve immediately.

Danuta's Rhubarb Cinnamon Muffins

Rhubarb may already be out of season when you make these, but you can buy it frozen. I couldn't resist adding this recipe since these muffins are soooo delicious! I want to thank my Reiki teacher for sharing this recipe with me. I did veganize it though!

Ingredients:

- 1 ½ cups flour
- 1 cup whole wheat flour
- 1 teaspoon baking powder
- 1 teaspoon baking soda
- pinch of salt
- egg replacer for 1 egg
- 1 cup soy milk (mixed with 2 teaspoons vinegar)
- ¾ cup brown sugar
- ¼ cup margarine (softened)
- 1 teaspoon vanilla
- 2 cups diced rhubarb

Topping Ingredients:

- ¼ cup brown sugar
- ½ teaspoon cinnamon
- 2 tablespoons finely chopped toasted pecans

Instructions:

In a bowl, combine flours, baking powder, and salt. Mix well.

In a large bowl, combine sugars, egg replacer, soy milk, margarine, and vanilla. Beat together well.

Add dry ingredients to wet ingredients and combine until just moistened. Stir in rhubarb.

Scoop batter into 12 non-stick lightly oiled or paper-lined muffin tins.

In a small bowl, combine brown sugar, cinnamon, and nuts. Sprinkle evenly on muffins and bake at 400°F for 20 to 25 minutes.

Amazing Blueberry Banana Muffins

Moist and tasty! These are so wonderful right out of the oven. They also stay moist for days.

Ingredients:

- 1 ½ cups sugar
- ½ cup margarine
- ¼ cup soy milk mixed with ½ teaspoon vinegar
- egg replacers (for 2 eggs)
- 1 teaspoon vanilla
- 2 cups ripe mashed bananas (about 3 bananas)
- 2 cups unbleached flour
- 1 teaspoon baking soda
- ⅛ teaspoon salt
- 1 cup blueberries

Instructions:

Heat oven to 350°F.

In a large bowl, mix the first 5 ingredients and blend until smooth.

Add flour, baking soda, and salt and blend for another minute.

Fold in blueberries and bananas.

Spoon into greased muffin tins and bake for 25 to 30 minutes.

Sprinkle with powdered sugar and cool.

Hearty Breakfast

Ingredients:

- ½ cup rolled oats
- ¼ cup flaxseed
- ¼ cup sesame seeds
- ¼ cup sunflower seeds
- ¼ cup walnuts or pecans
- ¼ cup raisins
- 1 to 2 tablespoon(s) sweetener of your choice
- 1 cup boiling water

Instructions:

The night before, cover the whole thing with boiling water and let stand overnight.

Next morning, heat it up in the microwave with a little brown sugar and syrup or honey.

Serves 2 to 3.

Buckwheat Pancakes

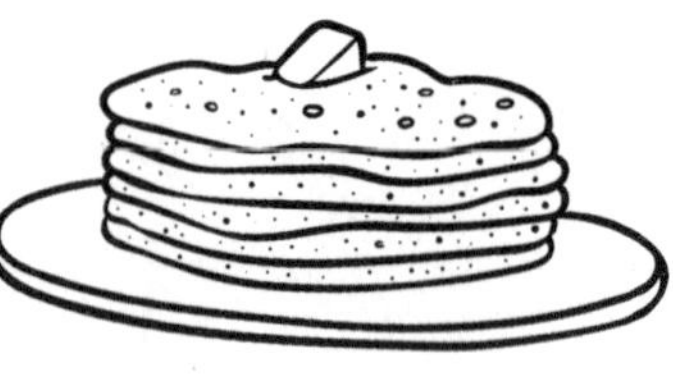

Ingredients:

- 1 ½ cup flour
- ½ cup buckwheat flour
- 1 teaspoon salt
- 1 teaspoon baking soda
- 2 teaspoon baking powder
- 2 cups soy milk (mixed with 2 tablespoons vinegar)
- egg replacer for 2 eggs
- ¼ cup honey or liquid sweetener
- 1 tablespoon melted margarine
- vegetable oil (to coat griddle)
- ½ cup toasted sunflower seeds

Instructions:

In a large bowl, sift together the flours, salt, baking soda, and baking powder.

In another bowl, whisk together soy milk, egg replacer, honey, and margarine.

Combine wet ingredients with dry, and stir with a wooden spoon until slightly lumpy.

Heat a griddle with oil, then pour ¼ cup batter (more for larger pancakes) onto the griddle, leaving 1-inch gaps between pancakes.

Lisa's Chocolate Chip Banana Oatmeal Muffins

This is one of my own creations. They are low fat if you don't add the chips!

Ingredients:

- 1 ½ cups oat flour
- 1 cup whole wheat flour

- ½ cup whole wheat flour
- 1 teaspoon baking soda
- 1 teaspoon baking powder
- ½ teaspoon cinnamon
- ½ or up to 1 cup of chocolate chips
- 1 cup applesauce
- 1 cup mashed ripe bananas
- ½ cup maple syrup
- egg replacer for 1 egg
- ½ cup soy milk
- 3 tablespoons oil

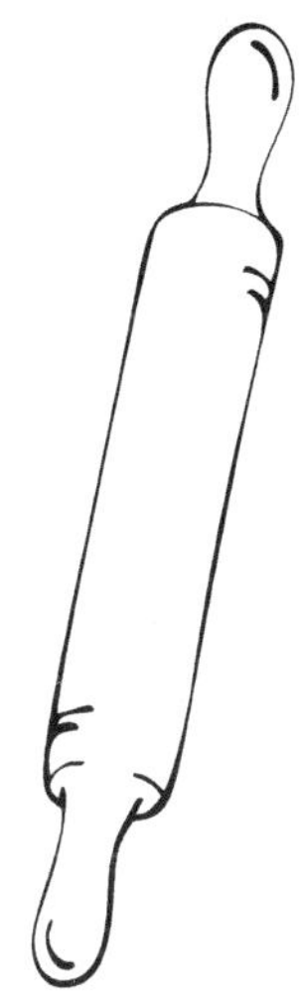

Instructions:

Preheat oven to 400°F.

Blend dry ingredients together.

Add wet ingredients and blend until just mixed. (Do not overmix.)

Fill muffin tins and bake for 20 to 25 minutes.

Makes approximately 14 to16 muffins.

Cinnamon Bread

Great breakfast or snack. Really simple to make and would make a nice gift too.

Ingredients:

- 2 cups all-purpose flour
- 1 cup sugar
- 2 teaspoons baking powder
- ½ teaspoon baking soda
- 1 ½ teaspoons ground cinnamon
- 1 teaspoon salt
- ¼ cup soy milk, mixed with 2 teaspoons lemon juice

- ¼ cup vegetable oil
- 2 tablespoons cornstarch, mixed with 5 tablespoons water
- 2 teaspoons vanilla extract
- 2 tablespoons white sugar
- 1 teaspoon ground cinnamon
- 2 teaspoons margarine

Instructions:

Preheat oven to 350°F. Grease a 9 x 5–inch loaf pan.

Combine flour, 1 cup sugar, baking powder, baking soda, cinnamon, salt, soy milk mixture, oil, cornstarch mixture, and vanilla in a large mixing bowl. Stir well.

Pour into prepared loaf pan and smooth the top.

Combine 2 tablespoons sugar, 1 teaspoon cinnamon, and margarine. Mix until crumbly. Sprinkle over the batter and swirl lightly with a knife to create a marbled effect.

Bake for about 50 minutes or until a toothpick inserted in the center comes out clean. Remove from pan and cool on a rack.

Basic Fluffy Pancakes

Who needs eggs for pancakes? These are wicked. Nice on cold weekend mornings with pure maple syrup or homemade jam!

Ingredients:

- 2 cups flour
- 1 teaspoon baking soda
- 1 teaspoon baking powder
- 2 cups soy milk (rice or almond)
- 2 tablespoons oil
- 1 teaspoon vanilla, optional

Instructions:
Mix dry ingredients, then add wet. Stir until just mixed—do not over stir. You can add fruit, nuts, or chocolate chips to the batter if desired. Pour into a hot pan and cook on medium heat until bubbles appear on top, then flip and cook for another minute or so.

Holiday Soups

Soup's on! Nothing is more comforting and soothing on a chilly night than a hot bowl of soup. Here are delightful soup recipes to warm your soul. All are easy and inexpensive to make!

Black Bean Carrot Soup

Ingredients:

- 1 medium onion, diced
- 2 cloves garlic, minced
- 4 medium carrots, diced in large pieces
- ½ teaspoon cumin
- 1 tablespoon chili powder
- ⅛ teaspoon pepper
- 2 cups veggie broth
- 2 cups crushed tomatoes
- 30 ounces black beans

Instructions:

In a little oil, fry onion and garlic for 2 minutes on medium heat. Add carrots and spices and cook for another 2 minutes. Add the rest of the ingredients, and simmer on low for 45 minutes. When soup is done, blend half of it in a food processor and return to pot. Serve with a dollop of soy sour cream and fresh bread. Note: I use 4 roma tomatoes and process them in a blender.

Carrot Ginger Soup

Ingredients:

- 1 tablespoon olive oil
- 2 pounds carrots, peeled and diced
- 2 cloves garlic, minced
- 2 tablespoons freshly grated ginger
- 1 onion, diced
- ¼ teaspoon turmeric
- ¼ teaspoon cumin
- ¼ teaspoon cinnamon
- 4 to 5 cups water

(You can decide how liquid-y you like it; personally, I love a thick soup)

Instructions:

Fry the onion, garlic, ginger and carrots in oil for 2 minutes. Add spices and fry for another minute on medium heat. Add water and stir. Simmer for 30 minutes. Take 2 cups of the liquid and process in a blender. Pour back into saucepan and reheat. Serve warm with fresh bread!

Tomato Lentil Soup

Ingredients:

- 1 ½ cups water
- ½ cup red lentils
- 3 stalks celery, sliced
- 2 carrots, sliced
- 1 to 2 teaspoon(s) fresh ginger root
- 1 small onion, coarsely chopped
- 3 ripe roma tomatoes, diced (or one 15-ounce can diced tomatoes)
- 1 teaspoon salt
- 2 teaspoons cumin
- 1 teaspoon allspice

Instructions:

In a large pot, bring water to a boil.

Add lentils, celery, carrots, ginger, and onion.

Reduce heat and simmer until lentils are tender, about 30 minutes.

Add tomatoes and seasonings. Simmer until heated through, about 5 minutes.

Makes 4 servings.

Gulyas Leves

A classic Hungarian soup, but this version has been veganized.

Ingredients:

- 3 tablespoons olive oil
- 1 onion, chopped
- 2 tablespoons Hungarian sweet paprika
- 8 ounces TVP granules
- 1 green bell pepper, chopped
- 5 cups vegetable broth
- 4 large potatoes, diced
- 2 large carrots, diced
- 1 tomato, chopped
- ½ teaspoon salt
- ½ teaspoon ground black pepper
- 2 tablespoons chopped fresh parsley

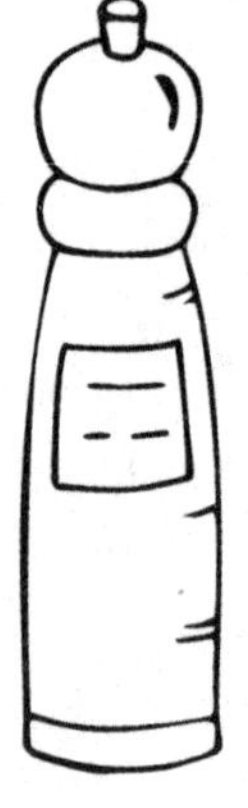

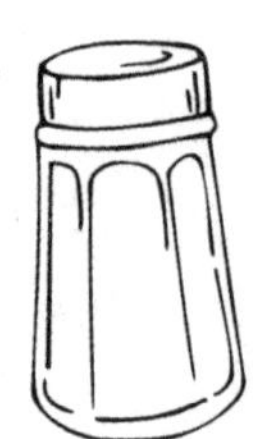

For Dumplings (optional):

- egg replacer for 1 egg
- 1 cup all-purpose flour
- ½ teaspoon salt
- 2 tablespoons water, as needed

Instructions:

In a heavy pot, heat oil over medium heat. Saute onions in oil until tender.

Add paprika, textured vegetable protein, and green pepper; cook and stir mixture until vegetables are coated with paprika.

Stir in broth or water, potatoes, carrots, tomato, ½ teaspoon salt, black pepper, and parsley.

Bring to a boil. Cover, reduce heat, and simmer until carrots and potatoes are almost tender.

For dumplings:

In a small bowl, mix together egg replacer, flour, and ½ teaspoon salt. Mix in enough water to have a smooth consistency; dough should be stiff and sticky. Spoon onto a flat plate and slice off small amounts into soup while it is simmering. Add to soup in such a way that dough does not land in the same spot every time. Continue until all mixture has been added to the pot.

Simmer until the dough is cooked (approximately 15 minutes).

Frugal Crockpot Tortilla Soup

Another house fave. Amazing!

Ingredients:

- 1 large (28-ounce) can of tomatoes
- 4 cups veggie broth
- 1 tablespoon cumin
- 1 tablespoon chili powder
- 1 teaspoon oregano
- 2 teaspoons onion powder
- 2 teaspoons garlic powder
- 2 to 3 cups crushed tortilla chips (use stale unsalted ones, if you have them) or 3 large tortillas (or 6 small)

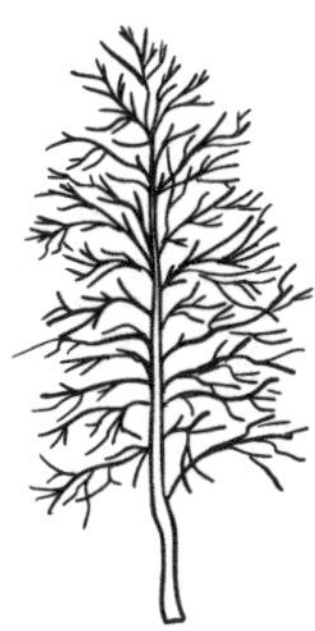

Instructions:

Put everything in a crockpot and cook on low for a couple of hours. Then blend till smooth. Place back in the crockpot and put on warm till ready to serve, or place in containers and store in the fridge.

Barely Anything Chili

I desperately wanted to make chili one day but had no diced tomatoes or tomato paste, nor soy ground. Here is what I did:

Ingredients:

- 2 tomatoes, diced (if you don't have this, try 1 can tomato soup or 1 ½ cups plain tomato sauce)
- ½ cup brown rice
- 2 tablespoons chili powder
- 1 teaspoon cumin
- 2 large garlic cloves (or 1 teaspoon garlic powder)
- green onions (or ½ cup chopped onions or 2 teaspoons onion powder)
- 1 teaspoon salt
- 1 teaspoon hot sauce
- 1 cup beans (I had some leftover kidney and black beans and used both)

Instructions:

Throw everything in a saucepan and cook on low till rice is cooked. This turns out pretty good if you spice it up well! It actually works well in a macaroni casserole: just cook some noodles and toss with this chili, and it makes a wicked dish that serves LOTS.

Harvest Soup

One of my latest concoctions. Very hearty! Good with biscuits too.

Ingredients:

- 1 large onion, diced
- 1 small squash (any kind), cubed
- 5 small potatoes, peeled and cubed
- 5 carrots, peeled and sliced
- 2 to 3 teaspoons curry powder
- 1 teaspoon cinnamon
- 1 teaspoon salt
- pepper to taste
- water

Instructions:

Fry onion in a little oil for a minute. Add potatoes, squash, and carrots. Stir for another 3 minutes. Add enough water to cover the veggies and blend in spices. Add more water until veggies are tender. Blend ⅔ of the soup until creamy, then pour back into pot and stir. Cook on low until done. Add more water if you want a completely smooth soup.

Dutch Split Pea Soup

Another one of my concoctions. This soup is easy to make, though feel free to play around with other spices. I've seen curry added to this soup before, though I didn't do it. If you don't wanna use the sausages, you can add a few drops of liquid smoke or spice it up with hot sauce.

Ingredients:

- 2 leeks, chopped
- 2 to 3 celery stalks, diced
- 2 large carrots, sliced or diced
- 1 onion, diced
- 2 Yves bratwurst veggie sausages or hot dogs, sliced thin
- 2 cups green split peas
- 8 cups water
- 1 teaspoon salt
- ½ teaspoon pepper

Instructions:

Fry leek, celery, carrots, onion, and bratwurst in a pan for a few minutes. Add peas, water, salt, and pepper. Simmer on medium-low for about 1 ½ hours. The longer you cook the soup, the better it is, so I usually let it simmer for 2 to 3 hours. But you can eat it after an hour and a half if you really wanted, as long as the peas are soft. You'll have to keep adding water too. The peas just become soft and mushy, so there will be no need to blend this soup. I find it's best to let it simmer at least 2 hours for best results, and my Dutch sweetie says simmering all day is best.

BruCee's Tomato Stew

When Brucee cooks, nothing is measured, so play around with the ingredients. This is so fricking good! Throw it all in a pot and heat. Serve with pita chips.

Ingredients:

- 1 28-ounce can crushed tomatoes
- some soy milk and water to liquefy

- 1 cup rice, cooked (so about 2 cups)
- cilantro (as much as you want! LOTS is good)
- 1 tablespoon dried coconut
- a couple green onions, chopped
- sea salt
- pepper
- some veggie meatballs

Lentil Soup

This is an easy hearty soup! Cheap to make too.

Ingredients:

- 1 onion, chopped
- 2 to 3 garlic cloves, minced
- 2 cups brown lentils
- 6 cups water
- 1 small can of tomato paste
- 4 bay leaves
- Hot sauce or cayenne pepper and salt to taste, optional

Instructions:

Fry onion and garlic for a few minutes in a little oil.

Add all other ingredients and cook on low-medium heat uncovered until lentils are tender.

You may need to add more water. Add pepper, salt, or hot sauce to taste.

You may process this in a blender if you want a smoother soup; just remove the bay leaves beforehand.

If you don't have tomato paste, I've used a bit of tomato soup in a pinch. You can also use a whole tomato or tomato sauce, but the paste is best.

Bruce's Broccoli Chowder

Comfort food at its best. Makes a large batch, so make sure you have lots of friends or a large appetite.

Ingredients:

- 1 small onion, chopped
- 1 celery stick, chopped very fine
- 1 medium carrot, sliced fine
- 1 broccoli stalk, chopped, stem and all—make sure to peel the stem first
- ½ cup or more of corn
- 2 medium potatoes, peeled and cubed
- ½ teaspoon cumin
- 1 tablespoon or more of basil
- 2 teaspoon salt
- ½ teaspoon pepper
- 1 liter plain soy milk (unsweetened is best, but it doesn't matter too much)
- ½ cup margarine
- ¾ cup flour
- ⅓ cup nutritional yeast
- a few pinches of turmeric for color, optional

Instructions:

In the largest pot you can find, melt a few tablespoons of margarine.

Add all the veggies and spices, and fry for a few minutes.

Add enough water to just cover the veggies. Heat on medium for about 5 to 10 minutes.

While the veggies are cooking, in another pot, melt margarine and add flour. With a fork, mix until you get a paste.

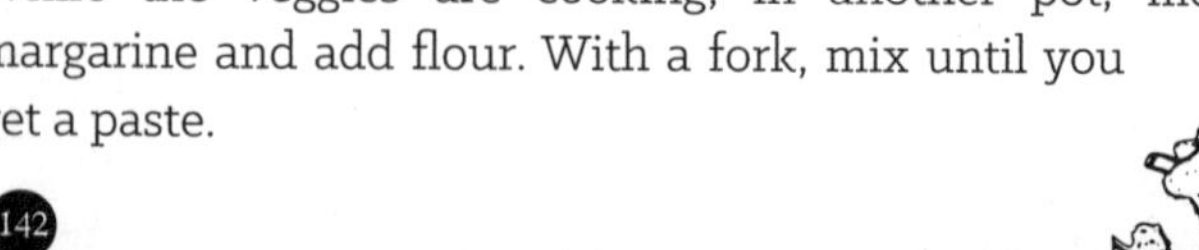

Add all of the soy milk and whisk. Add nutritional yeast and turmeric, stirring constantly until you get a thick sauce.

Once it's thick, pour it into the soup pot and stir well.

Lower the heat and simmer for at least 30 minutes to an hour. Add water as needed, perhaps 3 to 4 cups, depending on how thick you like your soup. Enjoy!

Holiday Entrees

Bean and Sweet Potato Burgers

One of my latest inventions from some leftover beans I had. This can serve up to 8 people and costs next to nothing to make, especially if you buy dried beans and soak them yourself!

Ingredients:

- 2 cups cooked beans (I used kidney and black beans)
- 1 cup mashed sweet potato
- ½ cup oatmeal flakes
- 2 teaspoon thyme
- 1 teaspoon sea salt
- 1 teaspoon hot chili sauce
- ½ cup minced almonds (optional, but I had them on hand)
- ½ cup corn

Instructions:

Mash beans with a fork, then add all other ingredients and blend well. Make patties and place them in the fridge for a bit (1 hour?). Fry in a pan until browned a little on each side. Makes 6 to 8 burgers.

Peanut Butter Banana and Molasses Sandwich

I made this up one day when I had a craving for all 3 ingredients. I threw in the seeds for a nice crunch! This is so satisfying and filling. Sometimes a half of this sandwich is enough to fill you up.

Ingredients:

- 2 slices whole wheat or bran bread
- 2 tablespoons unprocessed peanut butter
- 1 small banana, sliced
- 1 tablespoon (or less) of blackstrap molasses
- 1 tablespoon sunflower seeds

Instructions:

Spread peanut butter on bread. Add sliced bananas. Drizzle on molasses and top with seeds.

Sunflower Pesto Pasta

Pesto:

- 1 cup basil leaves, packed
- ½ cup sunflower seeds
- ¼ cup olive oil
- 2 tablespoons lemon juice
- 1 teaspoon salt
- ½ teaspoon pepper
- 1 tablespoon balsamic vinegar
- 12-ounce uncooked whole wheat or other pasta
- 1 ½ cups steamed broccoli, optional
- nutritional yeast

Instructions:

Place all pesto ingredients in a food processor or blender and blend until just smooth.

Cook noodles according to package directions.

When ready, add ½ cup of pesto and the broccoli to the pasta and stir well.

Serve and sprinkle with nutritional yeast.

Serves 4. Remaining pesto can be placed in the refrigerator and used for rice, pizza, or as a spread!

Brown Rice and Lentil Loaf

Ingredients:

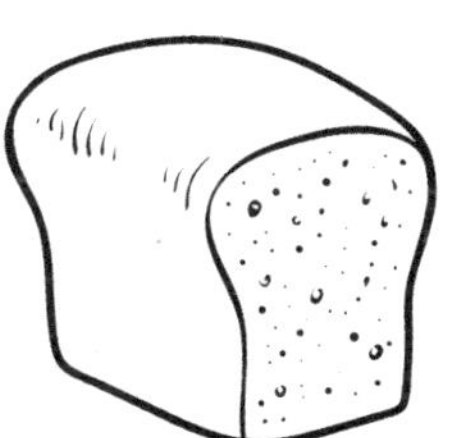

- ½ cup brown rice
- ½ cup brown lentils
- 1 large onion
- 2 cloves garlic
- 2 tablespoons oil
- ½ cup sunflower seeds
- 1 teaspoon basil
- 1 teaspoon marjoram
- ½ teaspoon thyme
- 1 teaspoon sugar
- ½ teaspoon salt
- 1 tablespoon soy sauce
- black pepper
- ¼ cup wheat germ
- egg replacer for 2 eggs
- 1 cup grated soy cheese
- ¼ cup sunflower seeds
- paprika

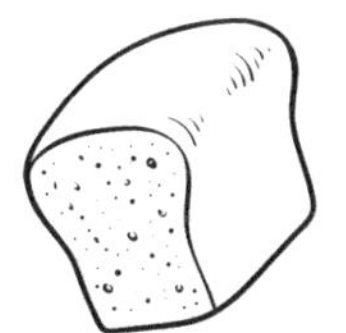

Instructions:

Cook the rice and lentils separately, or use 1 to 1 ½ cups of each precooked, if you have them on hand.

Chop the onion and garlic and saute them in oil until lightly browned.

Add the sunflower seeds and herbs and continue to cook for a few minutes.

Combine the next 6 ingredients and half of the cheese in a large bowl.

Stir in the cooked rice, lentils, and onion mixture, and mix well to combine.

Transfer the mixture to a carefully oiled or lined loaf tin.

Sprinkle with the remaining cheese, sunflower seeds, and a little paprika.

Bake uncovered for about 45 minutes at 180°C (350°F), until the center feels firm when pressed. Leave to stand for 5 to 10 minutes before turning out.

Serve with a selection of cooked vegetables or a salad of your choice. Leftovers are great cold.

Onion Quiche

For sauteing:

- 3 tablespoons olive oil
- 2 large onions, chopped
- 1 garlic clove, minced
- 2 tablespoons basil
- 1 tablespoon tamari or Braggs
- pinch of nutmeg
- salt and pepper to taste

In a food processor, combine:

- ½ cup cashew pieces
- 1 ½ cups silken tofu

- ¼ cup nutritional yeast flakes
- ¼ cup lemon juice
- 2 tablespoons tahini
- 2 tablespoons onion powder
- 2 tablespoons wheat germ
- 1 teaspoon salt
- ½ teaspoon garlic powder
- ½ teaspoon dill

Instructions:

Preheat oven to 180°C (350°F).

Bake a pie shell for 15 minutes. Remove from the oven and set aside.

Combine tofu mixture with onion mixture in a bowl. Pour into the pie shell and bake for 25 minutes.

Veggie Meatless Loaf

Ingredients:

- 2 ¼ cups cooked lentils (or one 19-ounce can)
- ¼ cup wheat germ
- 1 cup whole wheat breadcrumbs
- ½ cup cooked brown rice
- 1 minced onion
- egg replacer for about 2 eggs
- ¼ cup nutritional yeast
- 1 teaspoon dried oregano
- 1 teaspoon dried thyme
- 1 tablespoon tamari, soy sauce, or Braggs
- ¼ cup ketchup
- 1 tablespoon olive oil
- 1 teaspoon tabasco sauce, optional
- ½ cup tomato sauce

Instructions:

Coarsely mash lentils and combine with remaining ingredients.

Pour mixture into a loaf pan sprayed with non-stick cooking spray. Spread on tomato sauce and sprinkle with some nutritional yeast.

Cover with foil and bake at 350°F for 30 to 35 minutes.

Remove foil and bake for another 10 to 15 minutes or until the loaf is firm to the touch.

Makes 6 servings.

Quick Pumpkin Lasagna

Ingredients:

- 1 ½ cups pureed pumpkin
- 1 garlic clove
- 1 onion (diced)
- oven-ready lasagna noodles or cooked ones
- 1 ½ cups spaghetti sauce
- soy cheese

Instructions:

In a small saucepan, fry onion and garlic in 1 teaspoon oil. Add pumpkin and cook till the liquid has evaporated.

In a deep 9 x 9 glass dish or glass loaf pan, add a little sauce, then noodles, more sauce, ½ cup puree, and cheese. Repeat till all ingredients are gone.

Cover with aluminum foil. Bake at 400°F for approximately 45 minutes. Take foil off and bake for another 10 minutes.

Let cool a little before serving.

Spicy Sweet Potato-Bean Burritos

Ingredients:

- 1 teaspoon olive or canola oil
- 1 small onion, finely chopped
- 2 cloves garlic, minced
- 3 cups cooked beans, kidney or garbanzo
- 1 cup water or bean-cooking liquid
- 1 tablespoon chili powder
- 2 teaspoons prepared yellow mustard
- 1 teaspoon ground cumin
- 2 tablespoons Braggs or soy sauce
- 4 10-inch soft whole wheat tortillas
- 2 cups sweet potatoes, mashed and cooked
- 1 green onion, finely chopped

Instructions:

Heat oil in a saucepan over medium heat. Saute onion in oil until transparent. Add garlic and stir. Add beans, water, chili powder, mustard, and cumin.

Bring mixture to a boil over medium-high heat. Cover. Reduce heat to low. Simmer until beans are very soft, about 10 to 15 minutes. Stir in soy sauce.

Mash beans in the pot with a potato masher or large slotted spoon. Simmer, uncovered, over medium-low heat to cook away any excess liquid, about 25 minutes. Taste and add more seasoning if desired.

Preheat oven to 375°F. Spread about ⅔ cup bean mixture down the middle of a tortilla and top with ½ cup mashed sweet potatoes. Sprinkle with ¼ of the green onions. Roll up burrito, folding edges in from 2 sides to cover filling.

Repeat with remaining tortillas, bean mixture, sweet potato, and onions. Place burritos seam side down on a baking sheet that has been sprayed with vegetable cooking spray. Bake for 10 to 15 minutes or until burritos are crisp.

Sprinkle burritos with avocado and your favorite salsa as desired.

Makes 4.

Vegan Tourtiere

Ingredients:

- ½ cup raw millet, rinsed
- 2 tablespoons olive oil
- ½ teaspoon cinnamon
- 1 onion, finely chopped
- 2 cloves garlic, finely chopped
- 1 cup sliced mushrooms
- ½ cup sunflower seeds, whole or ground
- ½ cup oat flakes
- 4 tablespoons tamari
- 2 tablespoons nutritional yeast
- 1 teaspoon each of thyme, basil, parsley, and sage
- ¼ teaspoon cloves or allspice
- pinch of cayenne
- 1 cup vegetable broth
- 2 crust pastry

Instructions:

Combine rinsed millet with 1 cup of water in a medium-sized saucepan and heat to boiling. Reduce heat to minimum, and cook until millet has absorbed all the water, about 20 minutes. Remove from heat and let millet stand, covered, 10 minutes.

In a large frying pan, saute onion and garlic in the olive oil until onion is translucent. Add mushrooms, and cook for an additional 5 minutes.

Add oat flakes, cooked millet, sunflower seeds, spices, tamari, nutritional yeast, and vegetable broth. Combine well.

Pour the mixture into a pie shell and cover with the second layer of pastry. Bake at 350°F for approximately 25 minutes or until the crust is nicely browned.

Serves 8.

Bruce's Made-Up Pad Thai

Ingredients:

- 3 to 4 cups mix of veggies, including some onions
- 2 cloves garlic and 1 tablespoon ginger, chopped
- some tofu or beans (maybe a cup or less)
- 4 tablespoons peanut butter
- ¼ cup shredded coconut
- handful of raisins, pine nuts, and peanuts (and other nuts, if you wish)
- dash of mint
- ½ teaspoon dried red chili peppers
- ¼ cup soy sauce (or a bit less)
- 1 tablespoon molasses (or sweetener)

Instructions:

Cook the onions, ginger, and garlic in a little oil for a minute. Add veggies and tofu/beans. Add about ¼ cup water. Stir and simmer for 5 minutes. Add all other ingredients and mix well. Simmer for 10 minutes, then serve over hot rice.

Ethiopian Vegetable Bowl

Ingredients:

- 3 large onions
- 4 large carrots
- 3 potatoes
- ¼ each white cabbage
- 1 head garlic
- ¼ teaspoon ground ginger
- ¼ teaspoon turmeric
- ¼ teaspoon black pepper
- 1 teaspoon salt
- ¼ cup water

Instructions:

Peel and chop all vegetables. Heat oil in a pan and add veggies. Cover and saute for 2 to 3 minutes, then add spices. Cook on low for 30 minutes or more.

Stuffed Green Peppers

Ingredients:

- 4 green peppers
- 1 onion
- 1 pound ground round or 2 cups reconstituted TVP granules
- 2 cups canned tomatoes
- ½ cup rice, cooked
- Italian seasoning (oregano, basil, etc.) (as much/little as you want)
- 1 can tomato soup
- salt and pepper to taste

Instructions:

Fry onion in a little oil, then add ground round, tomatoes, seasonings, and cooked rice. Cut tops off peppers and clean out the insides. Place peppers in a deep dish pan and stuff them with the mixture. Mix tomato soup with ¼ cup water, then pour over green peppers. Cover with foil and bake at 350°F for 35 minutes.

My Version of Nasi Goreng

Yummy Indonesian dish that I adapted to make vegan!

Ingredients:

- 1 cup uncooked rice
- 1 onion (or 3 to 4 green onions, including the green part)
- 1 celery stalk, chopped
- 2 teaspoons grated ginger, fresh, minced
- 2 cloves of garlic, minced
- A few dashes of cumin and coriander (if you have it)
- 1 teaspoon red chili paste (found in Asian section of grocery store)
- ½ teaspoon sambal or more (spicy!)
- 1 tablespoons peanut butter
- 1 teaspoon sugar

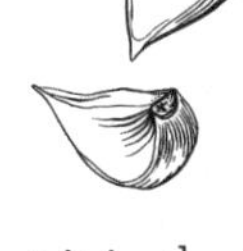

Instructions:

Cook rice as directed and cool. Sometimes, I put it in the freezer to speed that up. Put all other ingredients in a bowl and stir. Let marinate for 10 minutes or so. Heat a little oil in a wok and add contents of the bowl. Stirfry for about 5 minutes on medium heat. Add cooled rice and stir well until heated through. Serve hot with cucumber slices on the side and mango chutney if you have it.

Optional: Usually, Nasi has egg in it. If you have tofu on hand, crumble some up and add turmeric for color and a little salt to taste, then add to rice. I've also used small TVP chunks (½ cup soaked) for added protein.

Kick-Ass Coconut Curry

Ingredients:

- 1 can coconut milk
- 2 to 3 tablespoons curry paste (any kind you find in a jar: Madras, regular, etc.)
- 1 small onion, optional
- 2 cups of veggies or more (potatoes, broccoli, and carrots are good!)
- 15-ounce can of chickpeas or 2 cups cubed tofu

Instructions:

Fry onion in a little oil, then add veggies and fry for a minute or so. If you are using tofu, you might want to fry that along with the veggies. Add coconut milk, curry paste, and chickpeas (if using). Stir until well-blended. Cover and simmer on low until all veggies are cooked. Serve on top of basmati or jasmine rice.

Spinach Pasta

Ingredients:

- 2 cups uncooked penne (or any type of pasta you have on hand)
- ½ medium onion, sliced
- 2 cloves of garlic, minced
- ¾ teaspoon basil
- 1 green pepper, cut into strips
- 10-ounce box frozen spinach, thawed and drained

Instructions:

Cook pasta according to package directions, drain. Cook onion, garlic, and basil with olive oil in a skillet until onion is tender.

Add pepper strips and cook for 3 minutes. Stir in spinach and heat through. Sprinkle with nutritional yeast if you have it.

Microwave Lentils and Rice

Ingredients:

- 1 medium onion, diced
- 1 tablespoon oil
- 3 ½ cups broth or water + 1 teaspoon salt
- ¾ cup uncooked rice
- ½ cup dried lentils, rinsed
- 1 cup diced potato
- ¾ cup diced carrot
- ½ cup raisins
- ½ teaspoon black pepper
- ½ teaspoon ground cumin
- ½ teaspoon cinnamon
- ⅛ teaspoon ground cloves
- 1 cup diced bell pepper
- ¾ cup frozen peas

Instructions:

In a microwave-safe casserole, combine onion and oil. Microwave uncovered for 2 to 3 minutes, stirring once. Add all other ingredients except peas. Cover and microwave on high for 18 to 20 minutes, stirring occasionally. Stir in peas and cook for another 3 to 5 minutes.

Lentil Potato Burgers

Ingredients:

- ½ cup onion, chopped
- 3 stalks celery, chopped

- 2 tablespoons olive oil
- 2 cups cooked lentils, drained and mashed
- 2 cups mashed potatoes
- 1 cup bread crumbs
- 1 teaspoon dried parsley
- salt and pepper to taste

Instructions:

Saute onion and celery in olive oil until tender. Combine all ingredients, form into patties, and fry in a skillet over medium heat or bake at 350°F for 15 minutes on each side.

Lebanese Lentils and Rice

Ingredients:

- 3 medium onions, diced
- 1 ¼ cup lentils
- 1 ¼ cup rice
- ½ cup olive oil
- salt to taste

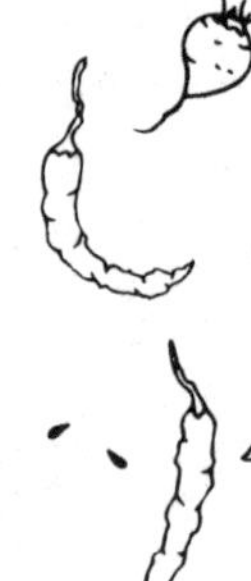

Instructions:

Fry onions in oil until golden brown. Add lentils to 5 ½ cups of water. Cook 20 minutes. Add rice and half the onions. Simmer until rice and lentils are cooked. Add remaining onions and salt to taste.

Homemade Tofu Scrambler Mix

The Mix:

- 1 cup nutritional yeast flakes
- ⅓ cup onion powder
- 4 teaspoons curry powder
- 4 teaspoons salt

- 4 teaspoons turmeric
- 4 teaspoons ground cumin

Instructions:
Mix in a DRY blender. Store in a covered jar.

To make tofu scramblers: Use ½ tablespoon mix for each 4-ounce firm tofu (mashed) or ¼ cup mix for each pound. Adjust for desired texture.

Yummy Tomato Beans

Ingredients:
- 2 cups navy beans
- 5 ½–ounce can tomato paste
- ½ cup brown sugar
- 1 onion
- 2 teaspoons vinegar
- 4 tablespoons ketchup
- ¼ cup margarine
- 2 cups water

Instructions:
Mix everything in a crockpot and cook on low for 10 hours. Great with rice or as a side dish!

Holiday Sides

Yummy Veggie Rice

Ingredients:
- 1 cup short-grain brown rice
- 2 cups water or veggie broth
- 1 small onion (diced)

- 2 to 3 cups veggies in season, lightly steamed

Instructions:

Place rice and water (or broth) in a saucepan. Bring to a boil. Then put heat on low, cover, and simmer until rice is cooked (30 minutes or so).

When rice is cooked, place in the fridge.

While rice is cooling, heat 1 tablespoon oil into a wok or large pan.

Add onion and fry on medium heat until translucent (2 minutes).

Add spices and stir for 1 minute. Add steamed veggies and stir for another 2 minutes.

Take rice out of the fridge and fry with veggies until heated.

You could add tofu or beans to this if you want to make this an entrée.

Shredded Sweet Potato and Raisin Saute

Ingredients:

- 4 cups shredded sweet potatoes (about 1 large potato, unpeeled and scrubbed)
- 2 tablespoons margarine
- ½ cup raisins
- 2 tablespoons maple syrup

Ingredients:

Prepare sweet potatoes in a food processor (shredding blade) and set aside.

Melt butter in a large, non-stick skillet. Add sweet potatoes and saute over medium-high heat for 3 minutes, stirring constantly.

Add raisins and maple syrup; saute 1 to 2 minutes or until sweet potatoes are tender.

Makes 4 to 5 servings.

Harvest Veggie Medley

Great holiday side dish!

Ingredients:

- 2 carrots, diced
- 1 cup diced turnip
- 1 cup diced sweet potato
- 2 medium potatoes, diced
- 4 to 6 tablespoons Braggs or tamari
- ¼ cup nutritional yeast
- salt and pepper to taste

Instructions:

Boil water, then add veggies.

Cook until VERY tender (this can take about 20 to 30 minutes).

Drain, then add other ingredients and mash with a potato masher or use a blender.

Walter's Roasted Potatoes

My honey makes the best potatoes! The paprika gives them a nice color too.

Ingredients:

- 5 medium potatoes,scrubbed and cubed—but unpeeled
- 2 tablespoons margarine
- 1 small onion, chopped
- 1 teaspoon paprika
- sea salt or Herbamare seasoning to taste

Instructions:

Boil water and add potatoes. Cook till just tender.

Drain and cool in the refrigerator. When cooled, heat up margarine on medium-high heat until bubbly.

Add onions and fry until translucent. Then, add potatoes and paprika.

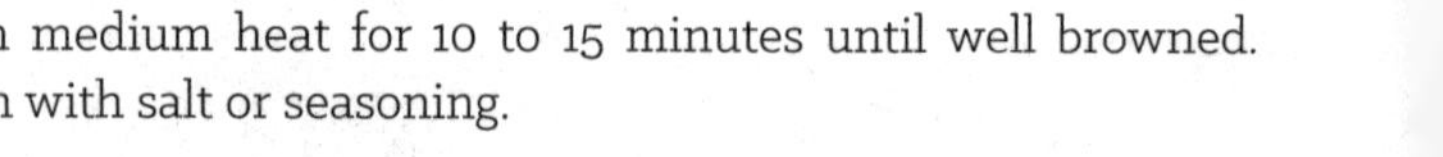

Fry on medium heat for 10 to 15 minutes until well browned. Season with salt or seasoning.

Microwave Caramel Buttercup Squash

This is yummy on its own as a snack or lunch.

Ingredients:

- ½ an acorn squash
- 1 teaspoon margarine (optional)
- brown sugar or demerara

Instructions:

Cut squash in half. Remove seeds.

Put some brown sugar in the middle (as much or as little as you want).

Dot the margarine on top and cover with cellophane wrap.

Put squash on a plate and microwave on high for 5 minutes. Let rest for a couple of minutes and dig in with a spoon! If you are sharing, scoop out the flesh and place in separate bowls.

Holiday Sauce and More

Tomato-Ginger Pasta Sauce

Ingredients:

- 2 tablespoons margarine
- 2 onions, chopped
- 2 tablespoons fresh ginger, minced and peeled
- 2 garlic cloves, minced
- 1 can (28 to 35–ounce) Italian crushed tomatoes
- pinch of sugar
- salt and freshly-ground black pepper to taste

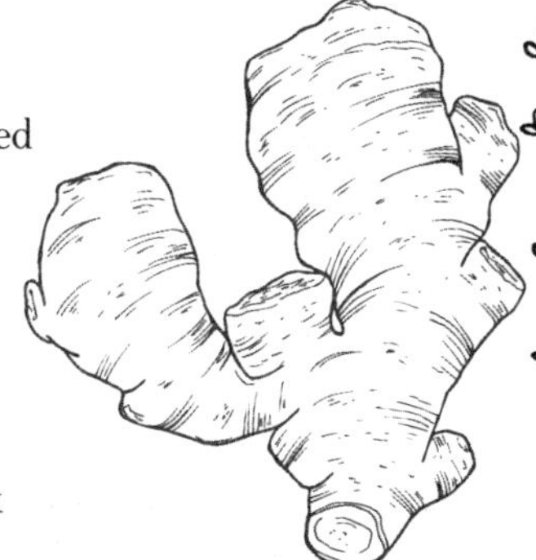

Instructions:

Melt the butter in a microwave-safe, 2-quart glass casserole dish with a lid, about 30 seconds on high.

Stir in the onion and microwave, covered, on high for 4 minutes. Stir in the ginger and microwave, covered, for 2 minutes longer.

Stir in the tomatoes and the sugar, if desired, and cook, covered, for 10 minutes. Puree in a food processor or blender until smooth.

Season with salt and pepper. Reheat for 2 to 4 minutes, if necessary, before serving.

Sauce freezes well. Makes 1 cup.

Roasted Red Pepper Hummus

Ingredients:

- 1 19-ounce can of chickpeas, drained

- ⅓ cup lemon juice
- ⅓ cup tahini
- 1 large red pepper roasted, peeled and diced
- 1 to 2 garlic cloves (roasted and minced)
- ¼ teaspoon dried basil

Instructions:

Put everything in a blender and mix until smooth. Let sit in the fridge for a few hours or overnight. Before serving, serve with pita wedges or use as a sandwich spread.

To roast pepper and garlic:

Preheat oven to 400°F. Quarter and seed pepper. Place pepper pieces and garlic cloves on a cookie sheet or pan and roast for 15 minutes. Let cool. Peel peppers and garlic when it's ready to use. (If you don't have the time to roast the pepper, you can buy roasted sweet red pepper in a jar. Use about ½ cup, drained.)

Crockpot Apple Butter

I have made apple butter a few times and found this method to be the best. You can just leave the crockpot on and not pay too much attention to it. This is my own recipe.

Ingredients:

- about 20 medium/large apples (chopped in quarters: not peeled or cored!)
- 1 cup apple cider vinegar
- 1 cup orange juice
- 2 teaspoons cinnamon
- ½ teaspoon cloves
- ½ teaspoon allspice

Instructions:

Place apples in a large stockpot. Add vinegar and orange juice.

Cook on medium heat until apples are tender.

Process apples through a food mill or sieve. (A food mill is much better, trust me!) You will end up with a lovely pinkish-colored applesauce.

Place applesauce in a crockpot and stir in spices. Heat on low setting for 8 to 12 hours. Feel free to stir every 1 to 2 hours, if you're around. If not, don't worry! The end result should be a really thick-looking applesauce.

Place in canning jars and put on lids, but do not tighten. Process in a water bath for about 20 minutes. Leave undisturbed for 24 hours. Tighten lids and label. Lids should be sucked in. If for some reason, some aren't, place the jars in the fridge and use within 3 weeks.

Banana Mush Spread

You know when bananas just aren't hard enough to slice because they'll squash? The kind you use to make muffins. If you want to use them but don't want muffins, here's how:

Ingredients:

- really ripe bananas
- brown sugar
- cinnamon
- lemon juice

Instructions:

Mash the bananas and add enough sugar and cinnamon to give it a nice taste. Stir in a few teaspoons of lemon juice, which will prevent the banana mush from turning black. This is good spread on toast or used to make a sandwich—even eat it on its own.

A good sandwich to make is banana spread stuff with peanut butter. MMMMMMMMM!

Canned Tomato Salsa

Ingredients:

- 1 28-ounce can diced tomatoes
- 1 jalapeno pepper
- 1 clove garlic
- 1 small onion
- ½ teaspoon salt
- 1 tablespoon vinegar
- ¼ cup green pepper
- a few dashes of cumin

Instructions:

Blend everything in a blender until veggies are chopped. For chunky salsa, blend veggies first, then add tomatoes.

Holiday Desserts

Candied Apples

Ingredients:

- 12 red delicious apples
- 12 wooden ice cream sticks
- 4 ½ cups sugar
- ¾ cup light corn syrup
- 1 teaspoon red food coloring
- 1 ½ cups water
- 1 cup chopped peanuts or candies

Instructions:

Line a baking sheet with parchment or wax paper. Set aside. Wash and dry the apples. Insert a stick into each apple, leaving about 2 inches for gripping.

Place chopped peanuts or candies in a deep bowl for rolling the apples.

Place sugar, corn syrup, food coloring, and water in a heavy saucepan over medium heat. Stir constantly while bringing to a boil. Cook until the temperature reaches 290°F.

Remove from heat and dip each apple in the syrup, coating evenly. Roll in peanuts or candies.

Place coated apples on the prepared sheet to cool for at least 1 hour before serving.

Carob Orange Cake with Creamy Carob Icing

Don't be put off by the orange juice in this recipe. You can barely taste it! This is a moist, light cake and is best iced with the creamy carob icing (see below).

Cake Ingredients:

- 2 cups spelt (or whole wheat) flour
- ⅓ cup carob powder
- 2 teaspoons baking powder
- ½ cup carob chips
- ½ cup maple syrup (rice syrup or barley malt syrup)
- ⅔ cup orange juice (use if using whole wheat flour)
- ⅓ cup canola oil
- 1 tablespoon orange rind (optional—only use if you want a more orangey taste)
- 1 teaspoon vanilla

Instructions:

Preheat oven to 350°F.

Mix dry ingredients in a large bowl.

Add wet ingredients. Stir until just mixed.

Pour into a lightly oiled 8 x 8 pan and bake for 20 to 30 minutes or until done.

Maple syrup will make a sweeter cake. I like using rice syrup myself.

Creamy Carob Icing Ingredients:

- ½ cup almond or cashew butter
- 3 tablespoons maple syrup (or honey)
- 3 tablespoons soy milk
- 3 tablespoons carob powder
- 1 teaspoon vanilla

Instructions:

Blend all ingredients in a mini food processor.

Spread on your favorite cake! This will ice an 8 x 8 cake.

Stuffed Baked Apples

Ingredients:

- apples
- dates (3 dates per apple used, chopped)
- 1 teaspoon of margarine per apple used
- splash of vanilla

Instructions:

Preheat oven to 350°F.

Core apples, but do not peel or chop!

Mix dates, margarine, and vanilla—and stuff apples with this mixture.

Bake for about 15 minutes or until apple is soft. YUM!

Vegan Fudge Coca Cola Cake

Ingredients:

- 1 cup Coca Cola
- ½ cup vegetable oil
- 1 stick margarine (½ cup)
- 3 tablespoons cocoa
- 2 cups sugar
- 2 cups flour
- ½ teaspoon salt
- egg replacer for 2 eggs
- ½ cup soy milk with 1 teaspoon vinegar
- 1 teaspoon baking soda
- 2 teaspoons vanilla

Instructions:

In a saucepan, bring Coca Cola, oil, margarine, and cocoa to a boil.

Mix the sugar, flour, and salt. Pour into the boiling liquid and beat well.

Add the egg replacer, soy milk, soda, and vanilla and beat well.

Pour into a greased and floured sheet cake pan.

Bake at 350°F for 20 to 25 minutes.

Crockpot Apple Peanut Crumble

Crockpots save TONS of energy and let you cook something when you're not around! I love this recipe because of the added protein.

Ingredients:

- 8 unsprayed apples, cored and sliced
- ⅔ cup brown sugar, packed
- ⅓ cup flour
- ½ teaspoon cinnamon
- ½ cup oatmeal
- ½ teaspoon nutmeg
- ⅓ cup margarine, softened
- 2 tablespoons natural peanut butter

Instructions:

Place apple slices in a crockpot.

In a medium bowl, combine the sugar, flour, oats, cinnamon, and nutmeg. Mix well.

Mix in the soft margarine and peanut butter.

Sprinkle over apples. Cover and cook on low for 3 hours or on high for 1 hour.

Serve warm.

Apple Cranberry Bake

A lovely and simple harvest delight.

Ingredients:

- 2 cups fresh cranberries
- 4 cups unsprayed tart apples, diced
- 1 cup sugar (cane or turbinado)
- 2 tablespoons margarine
- 1 cup quick oats
- ½ cup brown sugar or demerara
- 1 cup chopped nuts (walnuts or pecans)

Instructions:

Preheat oven to 375°F.

Mix fruit and cane sugar.

Spread mixture on the bottom of a greased 9 x 13–inch casserole dish.

Mix oats, brown sugar, and chopped nuts. Sprinkle this over the fruit.

Sprinkle the top of the casserole with margarine.

Bake for approximately 40 minutes.

Perfect Pumpkin Pie with Spelt Crust

Ingredients:

Topping:

- 1 cup chopped pecans
- 1 tablespoon molasses
- ¼ cup maple syrup
- 1 teaspoon arrowroot powder

Filling:

- 3 cups pureed pumpkin
- ½ cup maple syrup
- ½ cup soy milk
- 4 teaspoons canola oil
- 1 teaspoon cinnamon
- 1 teaspoon dried ginger
- ¼ teaspoon nutmeg
- ¼ teaspoon salt
- 2 tablespoons arrowroot powder
- 1 teaspoon agar powder

Crust:

- 1 cup + 2 tablespoons spelt flour
- 3 tablespoons oil
- 2 tablespoons cold water
- ¼ teaspoon salt

Instructions:

Topping: Combine all ingredients and set aside.

Filling: Combine all ingredients in a food processor and blend until smooth.

Crust: Combine all ingredients and pat into a 9-inch pie plate. (No need to roll this dough! Just pat it evenly in the pie plate by pressing with fingers. It won't look perfect, but that's ok!)

Heat oven to 350°F. Pour filling into pie plate and cover with aluminum foil. Bake for 50 minutes.

Take foil off and spread topping evenly over pie. Bake for another 20 minutes.

Let cool a few hours before cutting. (This pie tastes best the next day.)

Cider Pumpkin Bread

Perfect for harvest potlucks or to put in food gift baskets!

Ingredients:

- 1 cup firmly packed brown sugar (I use Demerara)
- 1 cup pureed pumpkin (use fresh, it's better!)
- ½ cup oil
- ½ cup apple cider or juice
- egg replacer for 1 egg
- 1 and ½ cups whole white or unbleached flour
- 1 tablespoon baking powder
- 1 teaspoon ground cinnamon
- ½ cup chopped nuts (walnuts or pecans—you can also use sunflower seeds)
- ½ cup raisins

Instructions:

Heat oven to 350°F.

In a large bowl, combine sugar, pumpkin, oil, cider, and egg replacer. Mix well.

In another bowl, combine all other ingredients and mix.

Add dry ingredients to wet ingredients and mix until just blended.

Pour into a lightly oiled loaf pan and bake for 50 to 60 minutes.

Make Your Own Pumpkin Puree

Instructions:

Buy a small pumpkin from your local farmers' market.

Cut in half. Remove seeds and "gook."

Heat oven to 350°F. Place pumpkin halves on a baking sheet, with a little water, face down.

Cook until you can easily pierce pumpkin with a fork. (This can take about 1 to 1 and ½ hours.)

Take out of oven and scoop out flesh.

Puree in a blender with a little water if needed. Voilà!

Tips:

Remember to use the seeds too!

Bake them for about 10 to 15 minutes at 400°F with a little sea salt. Mmmm.

Dirt Cheap Apple Dessert

Best if made when apples are in season and abundant. I've often found free apples on the side of the road where the trees don't belong to anyone. Some are sketchy but some aren't!

Ingredients:

- 8 apples, cored and diced
- ¼ cup brown sugar
- 1 teaspoon cinnamon
- 4 tablespoons butter
- ¼ cup oatmeal

Instructions:

Throw everything into a pot with a bit of water. Cook on medium heat until apples are tender. Throw in oatmeal, stir, and serve! If you have raisins, you can throw a handful in as well.

Pineapple Cake

This is a house favorite—VERY sweet! You might want to reduce the sugar if you don't like it too sweet.

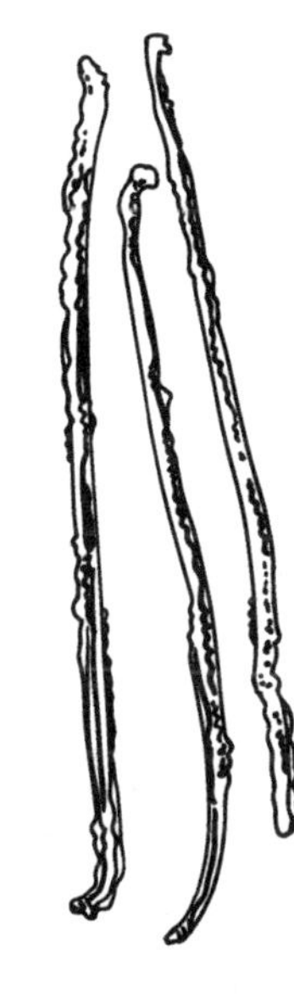

Ingredients:

- 2 cups flour
- 2 teaspoons baking soda
- 1 ½ cups sugar
- ½ cup silken tofu (or egg replacer)
- 1 19-ounce can crushed pineapple
- 1 teaspoon vanilla

Instructions:

Preheat oven to 350°F and spray a 9 x 13–inch pan.

Mix flour and soda in a bowl.

Mix sugar and tofu in a larger bowl until smooth.

Add flour mixture and mix, then add pineapple and vanilla.

Bake for 35 minutes.

Optional: Ice with non-dairy cream cheese frosting or sprinkle with coconut.

Spice Cake

This recipe might sound odd, but it's delicious and moist.

Ingredients:

- 1 10-ounce can tomato soup
- 2 tablespoons oil
- 1 teaspoon vanilla
- 1 ½ cups flour
- 1 cup sugar
- 1 teaspoon cinnamon
- ½ teaspoon cloves

- 1 teaspoon baking powder
- ½ teaspoon salt
- ½ cup raisins or chocolate chips, optional

Instructions:

Preheat oven to 350°F.

Mix wet ingredients, then add dry ingredients.

Spoon into a square or round pan.

Bake for 25 to 30 minutes.

Depression Cake

This is a recipe I found that is apparently from the 1930s. REALLY easy to make!

Ingredients:

- 1 cup packed brown sugar
- 2 cups raisins
- 2 cups water
- ¾ cup shortening
- 2 teaspoons baking soda
- 1 teaspoon salt
- 4 teaspoons ground cinnamon
- 1 teaspoon ground nutmeg
- 1 teaspoon ground cloves
- 3 cups all-purpose flour

Instructions:

Preheat oven to 350°F (175°C). Grease and flour a 9 x 13–inch pan.

In a saucepan, mix brown sugar, raisins, water, and shortening. Bring to a boil and boil for 3 minutes. Remove from heat and let cool.

In a large bowl, combine flour, baking soda, salt, cinnamon, nutmeg, and cloves.

When the raisin mixture is cool, add to dry ingredients and mix well to combine.

Bake at 350°F (175°C) for 30 to 40 minutes. Do not overbake or it will be too dry. Test after 30 minutes. A toothpick inserted into the center should come out clean.

Microwave Pralines

Ingredients:

- ¼ cup water
- 1 cup brown sugar
- 1 cup sugar
- ¼ cup corn syrup
- 2 tablespoons margarine
- 1 dash salt

Instructions:

Mix all ingredients in a microwave-safe or Pyrex bowl. Cover and cook for 4 minutes. Stir.

Cover again and cook for another 4 minutes. Stir in 1 ½ cups pecans, 1 teaspoon vanilla, and ¼ cup powdered sugar.

Mix for a few seconds, then drop quickly onto wax paper.

Let cool and wrap in cellophane bags or funky tins.

Chocolate Tofu Pie

I've made lots of versions of this, and so far, this is my favorite. VERY sweet, so it goes a long way.

Ingredients:

- 1 pound silken tofu (try to get as much of the liquid out as possible)

- ½ cup cocoa
- 1 cup sugar
- 1 tablespoon vanilla
- ½ tub Tofutti cream cheese, optional

Instructions:

Blend everything in a food processor and pour into a graham cracker crust. Bake at 375°F for 25 minutes, then refrigerate for several hours before serving.

Avocado Fudge

A house favorite—no one will ever know there's avocado in there!

Ingredients:

- 1 avocado, ripened
- ½ cup margarine
- 1 teaspoon vanilla
- 3 cups powdered sugar
- ⅓ cup chopped walnuts, optional

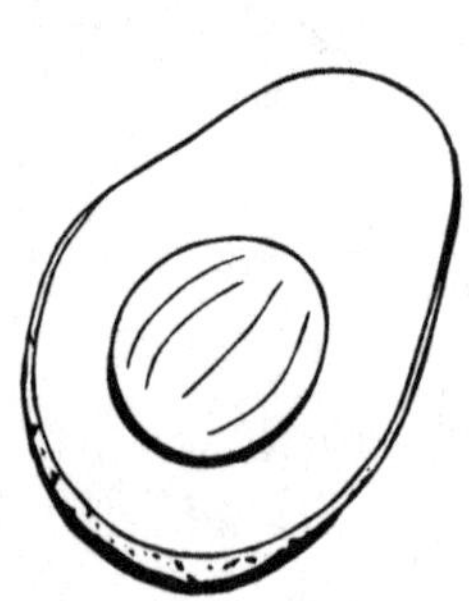

Instructions:

Melt margarine over low heat.

Puree avocado in a food processor or blender until smooth.

Return mixture to saucepan over low heat, adding powdered sugar a bit at a time until thick.

Transfer to a loaf pan and refrigerate until firm. Add walnuts if desired.

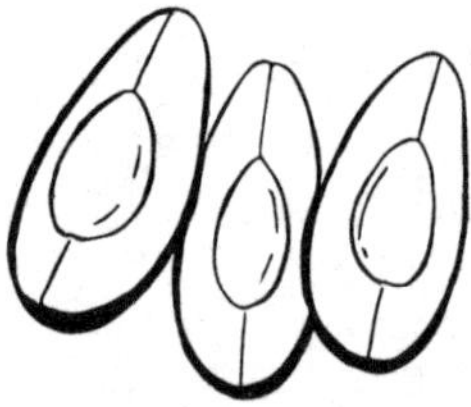

Lisa's Pumpkin Loaf

Another one of my concoctions. I always end up with so much pumpkin mush around harvest time!

Ingredients:

- 3 cups flour
- 2 teaspoons baking powder
- 1 teaspoon cinnamon
- ¼ teaspoon of spices like cloves, nutmeg, allspice, or ginger
- ¾ cup sugar
- ¾ cup soy milk
- 1 cup pumpkin puree
- 1 teaspoon vanilla
- ½ cup raisins or walnuts, optional

Instructions:

Preheat oven to 350°F. Mix dry ingredients. Mix wet ingredients, then combine. Stir in raisins or walnuts if using. Pour into a greased loaf pan and bake for 45 to 55 minutes or until a toothpick comes out clean.

Microwave Chocolate Fudge

This isn't fancy fudge, but it's easy and chocolaty!

Ingredients:

- 1 pound powdered sugar
- ½ cup cocoa
- ¼ cup margarine
- ¼ cup soy milk (or other alternative)
- 1 teaspoon vanilla
- ¼ cup chopped nuts (optional)

Instructions:

Blend sugar and cocoa in a microwave-safe bowl.

Top with margarine and milk but do not stir. Microwave on high for 2 minutes.

Stir well. Add vanilla and nuts, and spread into an 8 x 8–inch dish.

Cool in the fridge, cut into squares, and store in little boxes or wrap in wax paper.

Chocolate Peanut Butter Bars

SO bad yet SO good!

Ingredients:

- 2 ½ cups crispy rice cereal
- ¾ cup peanut butter (natural)
- 1 cup sugar
- 1 teaspoon vanilla
- 3 tablespoons margarine
- ¾ cup chocolate chips
- 3 tablespoons margarine

Instructions:

Place cereal in a large bowl and set aside. Butter an 8 x 8–pan and set aside.

In a saucepan, mix margarine, peanut butter, sugar, and vanilla. Cook on medium heat, stirring constantly, until hot and smooth.

Pour over cereal and stir well. Press cereal mixture into the pan.

In a small saucepan, melt chocolate chips and margarine on low heat, stirring constantly.

Pour over cereal and spread well. Refrigerate for one hour.

Gingerbread Cupcakes with Lemon Frosting

GREAT gift! Oh, and soooo good!

Cupcake Ingredients:

- 1 ¼ cups all-purpose flour
- 3 teaspoons ground ginger
- 1 teaspoon ground cinnamon
- 1 teaspoon baking powder
- ½ teaspoon baking soda
- ¼ teaspoon ground cloves
- ¼ teaspoon salt
- ¼ cup finely chopped crystallized ginger
- ½ cup vegetable oil
- ⅓ cup light molasses
- ½ cup maple syrup
- ¼ cup soy milk
- 1 ½ teaspoons finely grated lemon zest

Frosting Ingredients:

- ¼ cup soybean margarine
- ¼ cup vegetable shortening
- ⅓ cup confectioners' sugar
- ¼ cup soy milk
- juice of 1 lemon

Instructions:

Preheat oven to 350°F. Line cupcake tins with paper liners.

Sift together dry ingredients. In another bowl, whisk wet ingredients until emulsified.

Fold dry ingredients into wet ingredients, then fold in lemon peel and crystallized ginger.

Pour batter into tins, filling ⅔ full. Bake for 17 to 22 minutes. Let cool before frosting.

For the frosting: Cream margarine and shortening until smooth. Add sugar, soy milk, and lemon juice gradually, creaming until smooth. Refrigerate until ready to use.

Halifax Hurricane Recipes

This section was inspired by Hurricane Juan, which hit Halifax and surrounding areas in September 2003. We had a power outage, and I cooked all of these goodies on my BBQ.

Enjoy!

Baking Instructions for Your BBQ

As I quickly found out, baking IS possible on your BBQ!

Always have your BBQ on the lowest heat.

Place a large piece of aluminum foil on the grill (this prevents the bottom of your dish from burning).

Place your dish on the foil and watch carefully. If you have a super-duper hot BBQ, you might want to double or triple up on the foil!

Casseroles: Should be covered with foil.

Cakes: Should remain uncovered.

Crisps: Should remain covered for about 20 to 30 minutes after baking.

Note: Baking times are just a guideline. Always keep an eye on your food so it doesn't burn!

Potato Carrot Mush

(This recipe can be cooked on your BBQ or camping stove!)

Ingredients:

- 2 potatoes, washed and cubed
- 3 medium carrots, cubed
- 2 to 3 tablespoons nutritional yeast
- 1 to 2 tablespoon(s) margarine
- ½ teaspoon sea salt or herbamare seasoning

Instructions:

Boil water. Cook potatoes and carrots until they are quite mushy.

Drain and add other ingredients.

Mash with a potato masher. Serve hot!

Serves 2 to 4.

One-Pot Wonder

(This can be cooked on your BBQ or camping stove!)

Ingredients:

- 1 cup pearl barley
- 1 cup barley bulgur
- 1 cup brown rice (short grain)
- 1 large onion, diced
- 1 red pepper, diced
- 1 cup green beans, cut into 1-inch pieces
- 2 teaspoon curry powder
- 1 teaspoon turmeric
- salt and pepper to taste
- 7 cups water

Instructions:

Combine everything in a large saucepan.

Cook on low heat until water is absorbed and grains are cooked.

Feel free to substitute some of the veggies! Serves 10 to 12.

Millet and Rice Mash

- 2 cups millet
- 2 cups brown rice
- ½ cup lentils
- 3 to 4 carrots, diced
- 1 green pepper, diced
- ⅓ cup Bragg's or light soy sauce
- 9 cups water or broth
- 1 tablespoon herbamare (sea salt/veggie seasoning)

Instructions:

Throw everything in a HUGE stockpot and cook on low heat until the water has been absorbed.

Serves 12 to 15.

Pasta Bake

- 8 to 10 whole tomatoes, diced
- 1 small can of tomato paste
- 3 tablespoons olive oil
- 2 cups water
- 1 tablespoon Italian seasoning (basil, oregano, parsley . . .)
- 1 small onion, diced
- ½ cup nutritional yeast
- 1 package (450 g) of pasta (approximately 650 g cooked)
- bread crumbs + sea salt + sesame seeds (about 1 cup, combined)

Instructions:

Combine the first 6 ingredients and cook on medium heat until tomatoes are mushy. Mash with a potato masher and discard any large pieces of tomato skins.

Remove the cover and cook until some of the liquid has evaporated. Add yeast and mix.

Combine with cooked pasta. Spread in a 9 x 13–pan.

Sprinkle with crumbs, salt, and seeds. Cover with foil and bake.

Cover with aluminum foil and follow basic BBQ baking instructions at the beginning of this section. Bake til hot. Serves 12 to 15.

Apple Crisp

- 20 apples (diced and peeled) + 1 cup raisins
- ¼ cup flour
- 1 to 2 teaspoon(s) cinnamon
- ½ cup maple syrup
- 2 cups flour + 1 teaspoon baking powder + ½ teaspoon sea salt
- 2 cups rolled oats
- 1 cup sugar
- ½ cup margarine

Combine apples with ¼ cup flour, cinnamon, and raisins. Pour into a 9 x 13–inch baking dish. Combine all other ingredients and mix well. Sprinkle on top of apple mixture. Bake for 20 minutes. Serves 10 to 12.

Fruit Crisp Variation

- 2 cups strawberries, frozen/thawed
- 8 pears, peeled and diced
- 2 cups blueberries, frozen/thawed

- ¾ cup sugar
- 1 teaspoon cinnamon
- ½ cup flour

Combine above ingredients in a bowl and mix well. Place in a deep casserole dish. Mix the following in a bowl:

- 1 ½ cups rolled oats
- 1½ cups flour (combination of white and whole wheat)
- 1 teaspoon baking soda + ½ teaspoon sea salt
- ½ cup sugar + ½ cup margarine

Sprinkle on top of fruit and bake for 20 minutes on BBQ.

Moist Chocolate Cake

- 3 cups flour
- 8 tablespoons cocoa
- 2 cups sugar
- 2 teaspoons baking soda
- 2 teaspoons baking powder
- 1 teaspoon salt
- 2 tablespoons vinegar
- 10 tablespoons oil
- 3 teaspoons vanilla
- 2 cups cold water (or coffee)
- ¾ cup chocolate chips

Instructions:

Combine dry ingredients. Add wet ingredients and mix until "just mixed."

Pour into oiled pan and follow baking instructions in this booklet.

When cake has cooled, sprinkle on chips and place in BBQ uncovered for 1 minute.

Spread on melted chips. Feel free to sprinkle cake with nuts, seeds, or coconut!

Cookie Swap

I'm not quite sure where I got this idea but it's pretty unique (or maybe it isn't and I live under a rock). The idea is to invite five to ten friends over. Everyone must bring one dozen vegan cookies for each person attending the swap (not including themselves). It should be the same cookie recipe for each person, as it makes things less confusing. Along with the cookies, participants hand out a copy of their recipe to each person.

Make sure no one chooses a top-secret family recipe because sharing it is part of the fun! You can encourage your friends to be creative with the packaging too. Putting the cookies in a funky cellophane bag or a paper bag decorated with stickers or drawings. You can attach a simple tag that says, for example: "Jane's Vegan Bakery." A nice idea is to go to a shop where they sell fresh coffee beans and purchase a few of the paper bags they use for packaging. These are great for storing baked goods because they usually have a cellophane-type lining in the bag that keeps things fresh.

Some people use the cookies received to give as gifts, or eat them all themselves!

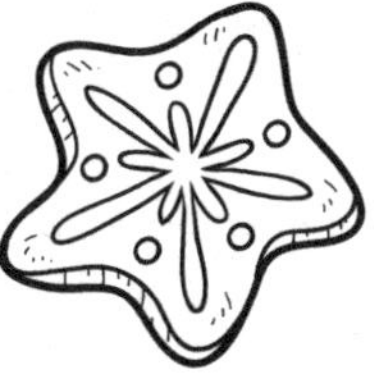

If you celebrate during the winter holidays and invite lots of people over, these cookie varieties are so handy to have! I believe the original idea was for everyone to come over and bake cookies at the host's home.

I don't know about you, but my kitchen isn't big enough for six people to bake in. Plus, do you really want to spend more than six hours watching other people bake?

HAPPY COOKIE SWAPPING! Here are some groovy recipes you can try for your swap party!

Fresh Ginger Cookies

These rock! They are so simple and inexpensive to make and are definitely in my top 3 fave cookies.

Ingredients:

- 2 ½ cups flour
- 1 teaspoon baking soda
- ¼ teaspoon salt
- 2 ½ tablespoons fresh ginger, minced
- ¾ cup margarine
- 1 cup sugar
- ¼ cup molasses (use blackstrap)
- egg replacer (for 1 egg)

Instructions:

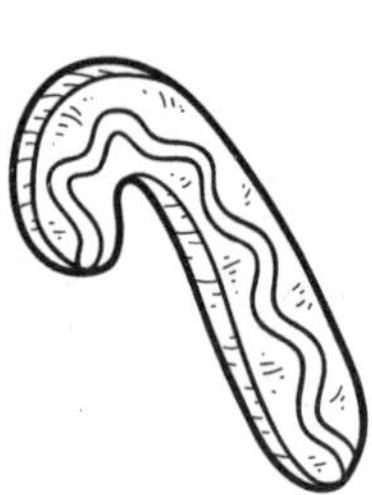

Combine flour, soda, and salt in a small bowl.

In a larger bowl, beat ginger, margarine, and sugar until fluffy (can be done by hand too).

Add molasses and egg replacer. Once mixed, add flour mixture and blend well by hand.

Chill dough for 1 hour. Form 1 ½–inch balls, roll in sugar (coarse turbinado or demerara is good for this).

Place on a greased cookie sheet 2 inches apart.

Bake for 15 minutes.

If you want this to taste amazing, please use FRESH ginger. The dried stuff won't make these taste nearly as good!!

Tightwad Bread Crumb Cookies

Ingredients:

- 1 ¼ cups flour
- 1 ¼ cups dry sweetener
- ½ teaspoon salt
- ½ teaspoon baking powder
- ½ teaspoon cinnamon (optional)
- ⅓ cup cocoa or carob powder
- ½ cup soy milk
- ½ banana (mashed) or egg replacer for 1 egg
- 2 teaspoons vanilla
- ⅓ cup melted shortening
- ⅓ cup applesauce
- 2 cups bread crumbs

Instructions:

Combine flour, sweetener, salt, baking powder, cinnamon, and cocoa in a large bowl.

Combine soy milk, egg replacer or banana, and vanilla in a smaller bowl. Add wet ingredients to dry ingredients.

Then add melted shortening, applesauce, and bread crumbs. Mix until blended.

Bake at 350°F for 15 minutes or until done.

Death by Chocolate Cookies

Ingredients:

- 2 ¼ cups flour
- ⅓ cup cocoa powder
- 1 teaspoon baking soda
- 1 teaspoon salt
- ½ cup sugar
- ¾ cup brown sugar
- 1 teaspoon vanilla
- egg replacer (for 2 eggs)
- 1 cup margarine
- 2 cups chocolate chips

Instructions:

Preheat oven to 375°F.

Combine 2 cups flour, cocoa, baking soda, and salt in a small bowl. Reserve an additional ¼ cup flour.

Combine sugars and mix. Melt margarine and add the egg replacer to sugar mix. Add vanilla.

Gradually mix in the flour mixture. Use reserved flour to thicken as needed. Stir in chocolate chips.

Refrigerate for 20 minutes or until dough is no longer tacky to the touch.

Drop rounded spoonfuls onto ungreased baking sheets. You might want to moisten your fingers to keep dough from sticking to them. Put the remaining dough back into the fridge.

Bake cookies for 8 to 10 minutes.

Date Filled Tahini Thumbprint Cookies

Ingredients:

- 1 cup dates
- ⅔ cup boiling water

Cookie:

- 1 cup tahini
- ½ cup oil
- ½ cup maple syrup
- 2 cups spelt flour (do not substitute!)
- 2 teaspoons vanilla
- pinch of salt

Instructions:

Preheat oven to 350°F.

Soak dates in water for 5 minutes. Puree dates in a mini food processor or mash well with a fork. Set aside.

Mix all other ingredients in a large bowl. Shape into walnut-sized balls.

Flatten with thumb and fill with date filling.

Bake for 10 to 12 minutes.

Makes 2 dozen cookies.

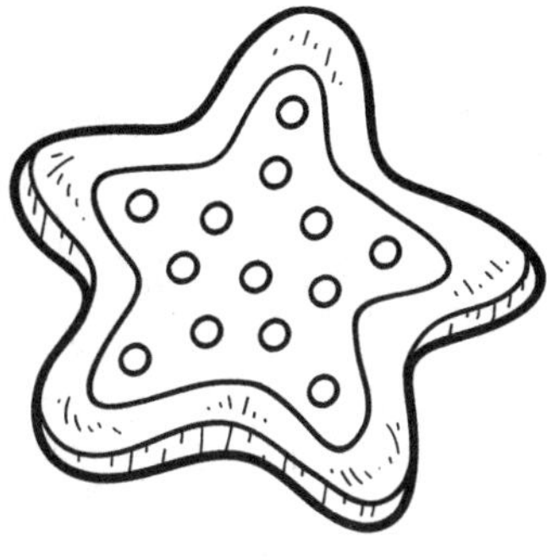

Beans

RECOMMENDED RESOURCES

- *How It All Vegan!* by Sarah Kramer and Tanya Bernard
- *The Garden of Vegan* by Sarah Kramer and Tanya Bernard
- *Vegan Freegan*, independent cook-zine by Jae
- *The Vegan Mary*, cook-zine by Till
- *The Voluptuous Vegan* by Myra Kornfeld
- *Vegan on a Shoestring: People's Potato Collective* (Montreal)
- *Herbal Teas* by Kathleen Brown
- *The Tightwad Gazette* by Amy Dacyczyn
- *Recipes for a Small Planet* by Ellen Buchman Ewald
- *The New Laurel's Kitchen* by Laurel Robertson
- *The New Moosewood Cookbook* by Mollie Katzen
- *The Uncheese Cookbook* by Joanne Stepaniak
- Veg Kitchen: www.VegKitchen.com

SUBSCRIBE!

For as little as $15/month, you can support a small, independent publisher and get every book that we publish—delivered to your doorstep!

www.Microcosm.Pub/BFF

Other books about Green Self-Empowerment:

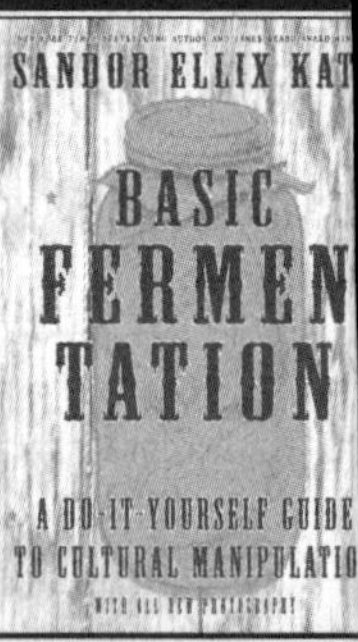